# THE
# ANCIENT WORLD
## OF THE
# BIBLE

## MALCOLM DAY

Viking

**Viking**
Published by the Penguin Group
Penguin Books USA Inc.
375 Hudson Street, New York, New York 10014, USA.

Penguin Books Ltd, Registered Offices:
Harmondsworth, Middlesex, England

First published in the United States of America by Viking,
a division of Penguin Books USA Inc., 1994

Conceived, edited, and designed by
Marshall Editions
170 Piccadilly
London W1V 9DD

Library of Congress catalog card number: 94–60486

ISBN 0–670–85607–X

Originated by Imago Publishing, UK
Printed and bound in Italy by Officine Grafiche De
Agostini–Novara

1 3 5 7 9 10 8 6 4 2

Executive Editor: Cynthia O'Brien
Managing Editor: Kate Phelps
Editor: Jill Laidlaw
Art Director: Branka Surla
Managing Designer: Ralph Pitchford
Designer: Nigel Hazle
Research: Simon Beecroft

Editorial Director: Ruth Binney
Production: Barry Baker, Janice Storr

Consultants: Dr. Albert Friedlander, Dean of the Leo
Baeck (Rabbinical) College in London and rabbi of the
Westminster synagogue, and Reverend Dr. Charles
Elliott, Dean of Trinity Hall at Cambridge University.

**ACKNOWLEDGMENTS**

Marshall Editions and Viking Children's Books would like to
thank the following artists for their contribution to this book:

**Robin Bouttell** (Wildlife Art Agency) 65t, **Harry Clow** 16–17c,
37b, 45t, 47t, 60b, 61b, 66–67c, 77b, **Joanne Cowne** 21br, 24t,
25t, 36br, **Mike Foster** (Maltings Partnership) 64–65b, **Richard
Hook** (Linden Artists) 10–11, 12c, 18t, 22b, 23t, 32–33c, 48–49c,
50–51b, 53t, 55cr, 77t, **Andre Hrydziusko** 14b, **Roger Kent**
(Garden Studio) 12cl, 13tr, 17br, 26–27c, 28t, 28b, 31b, 49t, 56b,
**Josephine Martin** (Garden Studio) all maps, **Steve Noon**
(Garden Studio) 62–63c, **Andy Peck** (Wildlife Art Agency)
28–29b, **Eric Robson** (Garden Studio) 8–9b, 21c, 42–43c, 52b,
57t, 69c, 76b, **Michael Roffe** 46b, 51t, 68b, 70b, 72–73c, 74b,
**Christopher Rothero** (Linden Artists) 25b, 30t, 38–39c, 44t,
46t, **Peter Sarson** 8t, 12–13b, 15t, 19t, 20–21bl, 26–27b, 29t,
29c, 32–33b, 33cr, 38–39b, 42–43b, 42t, 47b, 48–49b, 50t, 53b,
54–55b, 54cl, 55tl, 58–59, 62–63b, 66–67b, 71t, 72–73b, **Peter
David Scott** (Wildlife Art Agency) 40–41c, 44b, **Roger Stewart**
all parchment art, 30b, 31t, 33t, 45br, 52t, 61t, 64t, 71b, **George
Thompson** 6bl, 8t, 8bl, 19b, 21t, 23b, 24b, 34–35, 36bl, 37tr,
40bl, 55tr, 70t, 74t, 75b, 76t

# CONTENTS

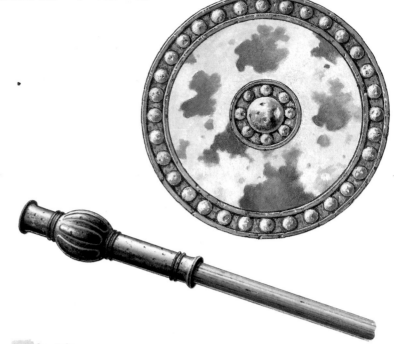

# INTRODUCTION

## *The story of how people came to live in a nation of God*

Between the ancient kingdoms of Egypt and Mesopotamia was a narrow strip of land. Desert lay to the east and the Mediterranean Sea to the west. Rivers, underground springs, and rain in the hills allowed life to flourish there. Bears and wolves roamed in the valleys and hills, and lions stalked through thick forests. Many people wanted to live there and fought each other for control of the area so that they could grow their vegetables, let their sheep graze on the hillsides, and build homes and villages with the forests' timber.

This book retells the story from the Bible of how one people, the Israelites or Hebrews, searched for this land, their "Promised Land," and made it their home.

The father of the Israelites, Abraham, received a promise from God that his descendants would form a nation. God said that he would lead his people to a land that would be their home as long as they obeyed his laws. The Israelites believed that any hardships along the journey to the Promised Land were because they did not follow God's commandments.

From their beginnings as wandering nomads, the Israelite tribes grew to become a powerful nation with a small empire under their kings David and Solomon, only to lose it all and be sent into exile.

The stories in this book bring to life the history of the Israelites. Their triumphs and disasters are seen alongside the everyday details of their lives and time.

*An Israelite high priest at the time of Solomon would have worn a breast plate (left) inlaid with precious stones. Every stone was inscribed with the name of the ancestor of each of the twelve tribes of Israel.*

*The people of the Bible lived in the area surrounded by the rectangle (right). All the historical maps in this book are located within this outlined area.*

EUROPE

NORTH AMERICA

ATLANTIC OCEAN

AFRICA

SOUTH AMERICA

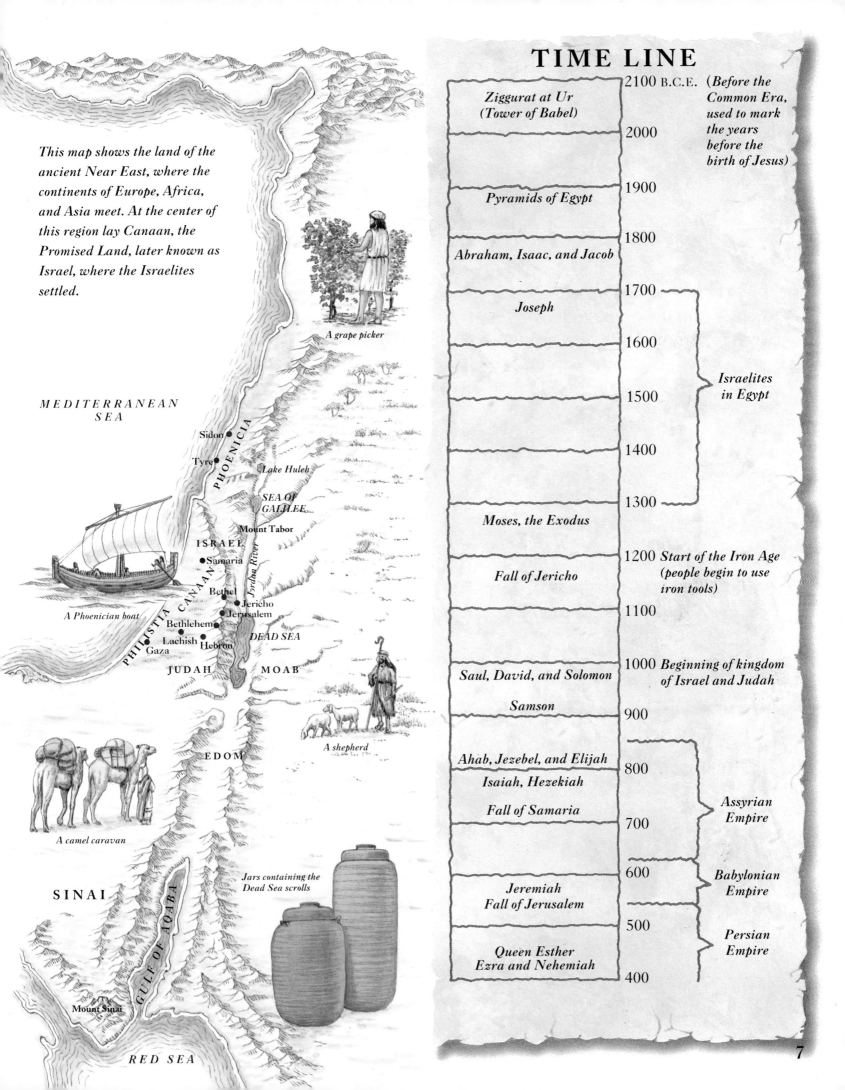

This map shows the land of the ancient Near East, where the continents of Europe, Africa, and Asia meet. At the center of this region lay Canaan, the Promised Land, later known as Israel, where the Israelites settled.

A grape picker

MEDITERRANEAN SEA

Sidon
Tyre
PHOENICIA
Lake Huleh
SEA OF GALILEE
Mount Tabor
ISRAEL
Samaria
Jordan River
Bethel
Jericho
Jerusalem
Bethlehem
Lachish
Hebron
Gaza
DEAD SEA
JUDAH
MOAB
PHILISTIA
CANAAN

A Phoenician boat

A shepherd

EDOM

A camel caravan

SINAI

Jars containing the Dead Sea scrolls

GULF OF AQABA

Mount Sinai

RED SEA

# TIME LINE

| | |
|---|---|
| Ziggurat at Ur (Tower of Babel) | 2100 B.C.E. (Before the Common Era, used to mark the years before the birth of Jesus) |
| | 2000 |
| Pyramids of Egypt | 1900 |
| | 1800 |
| Abraham, Isaac, and Jacob | |
| Joseph | 1700 |
| | 1600 |
| | 1500 — Israelites in Egypt |
| | 1400 |
| | 1300 |
| Moses, the Exodus | |
| Fall of Jericho | 1200 Start of the Iron Age (people begin to use iron tools) |
| | 1100 |
| Saul, David, and Solomon | 1000 Beginning of kingdom of Israel and Judah |
| Samson | 900 |
| Ahab, Jezebel, and Elijah | 800 |
| Isaiah, Hezekiah | |
| Fall of Samaria | 700 — Assyrian Empire |
| | 600 — Babylonian Empire |
| Jeremiah Fall of Jerusalem | |
| | 500 — Persian Empire |
| Queen Esther Ezra and Nehemiah | 400 |

7

# THE FIRST PEOPLE

*Stories of how people came to spread across the Earth*

Pomegranates

Figs

## Adam and Eve

God created Heaven and Earth and all kinds of birds and animals to fill the world. The stars and moon shone in the sky and gave light at night. The sun shone and gave light during the day. But there was nobody to look after God's creation, and so God made a man out of the dust and breathed life into his nostrils. God called the man Adam.

God planted a garden in the eastern part of the land of Eden, with a river flowing through it that divided into four streams. God put fruit, trees, and plants in Eden for Adam to eat and enjoy. The Garden of Eden was so beautiful that it has been called paradise—a place

people think is like heaven. God gave the garden to Adam to look after. But in the middle of the garden God planted two trees: the tree of life and the tree of the knowledge of good and evil. If Adam ate the fruit of these trees he would die.

God brought all the world's animals to Eden for Adam to name and so that he could see if any would be suitable as a companion. None of them was, so when Adam was in a deep sleep, God took one of his ribs and made a woman out of it.

One of the creatures God had brought to the garden was the snake. The snake knew about the fruit from the trees in the middle of Eden. The woman told the

A turtle dove

*Four rivers flowed through the Garden of Eden: the Pishon, the Gihon, the Tigris, and the Euphrates. These rivers made the land very fertile so that many different plants and animals thrived there. The Tigris and the Euphrates rivers still exist today, but because the Pishon and the Gihon have disappeared, we do not know where the Garden of Eden was—although it was probably in Mesopotamia, an area now covered by the country of Iraq.*

*The fruit of the tree of knowledge is often thought to have been an apple, but it is much more likely that the fruit would have been a pomegranate, since they are more common in this area than apples.*

Olives

*An early picture of Adam and Eve and the tree of life from a Mesopotamian cylinder seal.*

snake that she was not allowed to eat the fruit. The snake burst out laughing and said, "Of course you will not die if you eat this fruit! God knows that if you do, you will become like God and will know the difference between good and evil." The woman saw how delicious the fruit looked.

She plucked one from the tree and ate some, and then gave it to Adam to eat.

When the evening came, Adam and the woman heard God in the garden. Suddenly they realized that they were naked. They were afraid and hid among the trees. But God called for them, so they came out and told him what had happened.

God was furious. The snake, the man, and the woman were all punished for disobeying God. The snake would now crawl on its belly; the woman would give birth to children in great pain; and the man would work hard on the land all his life.

Adam now named the woman Eve. God still loved the first people and saw that they were clothed before he sent them out of the Garden of Eden into the world.

# Cain and Abel

Now that Adam and Eve no longer lived in the Garden of Eden, they felt alone. They knew they had a lot of hard work to do to feed and look after themselves. After a while they had a son named Cain who became a farmer, like his father. Later, a second son was born, named Abel, who became a shepherd.

The first people believed that everything was created by God and that some of what he provided should be returned to him. So to thank God for the vegetables that had grown, Cain built an altar out of stones and put the best crops on the top to offer to God. Abel also built a stone altar, but he took a

*Shepherds and farmers believed God owned the soil and all that grew in it. It was their duty to offer back to God some of what he had allowed them to grow.*

young lamb from his flock and put it on the altar as an offering to God.

God was pleased with the lamb that Abel had given as an offering. But he was not as pleased with Cain's offering. Cain was angry that God should prefer his brother's offering when he had worked so hard on the land to grow his vegetables. God then said to Cain, "If you do what is right, won't you be accepted? If you do not do what is right, then watch out, because you will make trouble for yourself."

Now Cain was not only angry but also very jealous of his brother. "Let's go out to the field," he said to Abel one day, pretending to be friendly. While they were out in the field Cain could not control his anger any longer, and he attacked and killed his

*In biblical times, most people lived by farming the land. Farmers used simple tools such as plows to help them. A plow was made of wood and iron and was used to break up the soil and mix the seeds into the earth. It would have been pulled by oxen or donkeys and steered by the farmer.*

brother. Cain's anger turned to fear as he heard God call, "Where is your brother Abel?" "I don't know," replied Cain in a panic, "Am I my brother's keeper?" "What have you done?" God asked. But he knew exactly what had happened. As Abel's blood seeped into the ground, Cain realized his terrible crime and held his head in his hands in despair. "When you work the ground," God told him, "it will no longer give you crops. You will be a restless wanderer on earth."

Cain was desperate. How was he going to survive? He could no longer be a farmer, the only work he knew, and he was afraid that anyone who recognized him would try to kill him. But God protected Cain by putting a mark on him. Anyone who found him

*Cain's descendants became metalworkers. This coppersmith is making a pattern on the side of a copper pot using a special tool. He would have made kitchen utensils such as frying pans and pots, as well as weapons.*

*A shepherd looked after his flock, protecting it from attack by wild animals such as wolves. The flock would have included goats as well as sheep. The sheep were kept to supply people with wool and meat. The goats provided milk, hair, and skins.*

would know that God protected him and would not try to seek revenge for the jealous murder of his brother Abel.

Cain became the founder of the Kenite clan, who wandered through the deserts of Arabia on donkeys. They made tools out of iron and copper and musical instruments like flutes and harps. Most of the Kenite people lived in tents and tended cattle.

These traveling metalworkers were recognized by a metal badge worn on their foreheads. This badge may have been the "mark" that God gave to Cain. It told other people that they were craftsmen and not rulers of the land. The name Cain means smith or metalworker.

The Kenites later settled in the land which God gave to Moses and the Israelites, known as the "Promised Land." They became neighbors and rivals of the Israelites.

# Noah's Ark

One of the many thousands of descendants of Adam was Noah. He was a good man who lived in an evil time. When God saw how wicked his world had become he was sorry to have created it. So he decided to flood the earth and destroy it all! He would spare only the faithful Noah and his family.

God told Noah to build an Ark, in which his family and the animals God provided would be safe from the flood. Noah and his three sons, Shem, Ham, and Japheth, set to building the boat.

After many years the Ark was ready. Noah took one pair of every animal, and seven extra pairs of birds and of animals such as lambs, to provide food for Noah's family. For seven days Noah and his sons herded all the animals into the Ark until finally all were aboard. Just then the first drops of rain began to fall—and they kept falling for forty days and forty nights, and the Ark floated on the flood water.

After the rain, when the water level had begun to drop again, a jolt at the bottom of the Ark told Noah there was land beneath them. Noah sent out a raven, thinking that if it did not return, it would have found land. But the raven came back. After a while Noah sent out a dove on the same mission. This time the bird returned with an olive leaf in its beak. The next time the dove was

*The Ark was built from "gopher wood," which comes from cypress trees and is like pine.*

## BUILDING A BOAT

*The units of measurement used in this time included the cubit and the span. A cubit was the length of a man's arm from the elbow to the tip of his longest finger. A span was the width of his hand.*

*A span*

*A cubit*

*To cut planks of wood two men used a giant saw in a saw-pit. The man in the pit pushed the saw up through the trunk and the other man pushed it down.*

**BUILDING TOOLS**

*A chisel*

*A mallet*

*A bodkin*

sent out it did not return and Noah knew that it was time to leave the Ark.

When the Ark had come to rest on the side of a mountain called Ararat, Noah led out all the animals: the birds, insects, and other creatures. God blessed Noah and his family and told them to make a new beginning. God showed Noah the sky and told him that a rainbow would be the sign of God's promise never to let a flood come to destroy life on earth again.

*Mount Ararat is 17,000 feet high, the highest mountain in the Ararat Range in eastern Turkey.*

*The Bible says that the Ark was a rectangular boat three stories high with only one entrance on one side. It was 300 cubits (510 feet) long, 30 cubits (51 feet) high, and 50 cubits (85 feet) wide.*

*This pot contains pitch, a type of tar. Boats were made watertight by filling the gaps between planks of wood with flax and pitch.*

*Sails were sewn by hand from the finest Egyptian linen—a type of cloth made of fibers taken from the flax plant.*

*A saw*

*An ax*

# The Tower of Babel

After the flood, there were no more misunderstandings among people. But the land was not their home and they sadly wandered the world in search of a better place, a land they could call their own. They finally came to Babylon on the Euphrates River. Here they decided to build a city with a tall tower that would reach up high into the sky. They wanted to create something that they could be proud of and that they could call their own.

They organized themselves into teams of builders. Some people made the bricks and others made the tar to stick the bricks together. Others helped to carry the building materials—there was no shortage of people to help.

God saw what was happening and was not happy. People were trying to reach Heaven by their own means. "I will confuse their language and scatter them over the whole world," God decided. He called the tower Babel, which means "to confuse."

Arguments broke out between people. They were not able to work together because they could no longer understand each other. They fought, stopped building the city, and moved away to find new places to live. From then on people in different parts of the world spoke different languages.

EUROPE

AFRICA

*Large towers like the one at Babylon were quite common in Mesopotamia. There were more than thirty at this time (around 2000 B.C.E.). The towers were called ziggurats. The Mesopotamians built them in order to make contact with their gods and held religious festivals at them.*

*The ziggurat at Ur (right) was dedicated to the moon god. The king and his royal priest would climb the stairways up the sides of the ziggurat. At the top there would be a shrine where they made offerings to the god.*

According to the Bible, Noah's three sons, Shem, Ham, and Japheth, became the ancestors of all the people in the world. Shem was the first of the ancient peoples who lived in the Near East and are known as Semites. His descendants included Abraham and Moses.

The Egyptians and Africans came from Ham. Japheth's descendants migrated to Europe, Asia Minor, Central Asia, and India.

This Egyptian wall painting shows a group of Semitic people visiting Egypt.

A map showing the migration of peoples from Mesopotamia to Europe, Africa, Arabia, Asia Minor, and Asia. From these peoples the different cultures of the world arose, including the pharaohs of Egypt, the Hittites of Asia Minor, and the Aryans of India.

A Hittite warrior

BLACK SEA

CASPIAN SEA

ion Gate in
lycenae

ASIA MINOR

ARARAT MOUNTAINS

Tigris River

MESOPOTAMIA

A Phoenician ship

A ziggurat

MEDITERRANEAN SEA

Babylon
Ur

A reed house

A camel caravan

ASIA

Euphrates River

CANAAN

THE PERSIAN GULF

Travelers

SINAI

EGYPT

RED SEA

A nomads' camp

The pyramids

Nile River

ARABIA

A reed boat

An Egyptian
pharaoh

An Egyptian ship

AFRICA

# Abraham's Family

*Stories of the first Israelites*

## Sodom and Gomorrah

Abraham, a descendant of Noah's son Shem, was the father of God's chosen people, the Israelites. One day Abraham's nephew, Lot, was sitting at the gateway to the city of Sodom when two angels arrived. Lot greeted them and invited them to dinner at his house. The angels accepted but were very cautious because they had heard that the men of the city were evil.

In the evening, a crowd gathered outside Lot's house demanding to take away the angels. Lot tried to reason with them, but the men threatened to break down his door. Afraid of a riot, the angels pulled Lot inside and cast a spell of blindness on the violent mob.

The angels knew that it was only a matter of time before the mob broke into the house. "Hurry!" they said. "Get out of this place. God is about to destroy this wicked city." Lot quickly passed the angels' message on to his two daughters and sons-in-law.

When dawn was about to break, the angels secretly showed Lot's family the way to escape from the city. "Flee to the mountains," the angels told Lot, "but whatever

*An earthquake, such as the one depicted here, may have caused the destruction of Sodom and Gomorrah. The cities were situated to the south of the Dead Sea and lay in fertile plains of lush green forests and vegetation. It is possible that great boulders of salt from the Dead Sea—which is very salty—fell into the cracks in the earth and were hurled up into the air when they met the heat in the cracks. Today, submerged forests lie at the southern end of the Dead Sea. It is thought that the whole area probably sank below sea level after an earthquake.*

16

you do, don't look back." Lot set off with his family, afraid of what was going to happen next.

When the sun had risen, Lot's family had traveled a fair distance out of the city. Strange weather suddenly came over the land. It seemed to be raining; but it was not water. Great balls of burning sulphur fell from the sky over the twin cities of Sodom and Gomorrah, which burst into flames. A terrible fire blazed across the plain. The air was thick with black smoke, like the smoke from a furnace. Although Lot and his family were now a safe distance from the cities, Lot's wife forgot the angels' warning and looked back at the catastrophe. She was instantly turned into a pillar of salt.

The next day the smoke was still rising into the air as Abraham came to comfort his nephew Lot who had lost his wife in the escape from Sodom and Gomorrah.

*At the southern end of the Dead Sea are salt pillars that glisten in the water as they catch the sun's rays. They look like floating statues. The Dead Sea is a lake partly in modern-day Israel and partly in modern-day Jordan.*

# The Promise to Abraham

When Abraham was seventy-five years old God told him to leave his home in Haran and go in search of another land. He went south to Canaan with his wife Sarah, his nephew Lot, and all his possessions.

Times were hard: a famine forced Abraham to go to Egypt in search of food. When he returned to Canaan he and his family got involved in battles between rival kings who fought over the land. At one time Abraham had to rescue Lot, who was taken hostage.

One night Abraham lay worrying about his life: why had he left behind his livelihood and comfortable home? Life as a nomad was dangerous now,

*Nomads like Abraham's family lived in tents. The tents were often made out of sheets of woven black goat hair five or six feet wide. The goat-hair cloth was draped across several poles and the ends were pegged into the ground like a modern-day tent.*

*Abraham was born in Ur in Mesopotamia. He then settled in Haran, farther north. On God's command he and his family traveled to Canaan. Later Abraham went to Egypt in search of food and then returned home to Canaan.*

ASIA MINOR

*Beehive houses*

Haran

MESOPOTAMIA

*Euphrates River*

*Tigris River*

MEDITERRANEAN SEA

*A ziggurat*

Babylon

CANAAN

DEAD SEA

Ur

EGYPT

*A nomads' tent*

THE PERSIAN GULF

AFRICA

*The pyramids*

*An oasis*

*Nile River*

RED SEA

with neither a house nor land to farm. And he had no heir. Would his wife Sarah ever have a child?

It was while he was thinking about these difficult questions that Abraham suddenly felt that God was there. "Do not be afraid," said a voice. "Look up at the heavens and count the stars, if you can, for you will have as many descendants as there are stars." As impossible as this seemed to Abraham, he believed it. Abraham fell into a deep sleep and dreamed that his descendants would be strangers in a foreign country and slaves for four hundred years. Then God said, "I will give your descendants this land: from the Nile River in Egypt to the great Euphrates River."

However, the problem of having no children was still not solved. Because Sarah could not have children, she told Abraham to have a child with Hagar, her maidservant. Hagar gave birth to a boy called Ishmael, and Sarah felt sadder as she grew older, knowing that she would never have a child.

*A water carrier*

*A water carrier was made out of a complete animal skin.*

*Sandals*

*Sandals were worn by all people, rich and poor.*

*This small statue is of an Egyptian maidservant (2134–1991 B.C.E). The maid wears a wig, as was common at the time, and carries a basket on her head and a bird in her free hand. Egyptian maids like Hagar were in great demand.*

One day three visitors came to Abraham's tent. Abraham and Sarah cooked them a meal. After dinner, when the men were talking alone, the visitors predicted that by the same time the following year Sarah would have a child. Sarah overheard and laughed, though she hoped it would come true.

Sure enough, before the year was out Sarah gave birth to a son whom she named Isaac, which means "laughter." Abraham held a great feast to celebrate. During the feast, Ishmael started poking fun at his half brother. This made Sarah furious and she told Abraham to send Ishmael and his mother away.

With a sad heart Abraham sent them away with some food and water. Their supplies were soon used up and Hagar began to cry because she knew her son was going to die. As she sat on the ground a voice spoke to her. "Do not be afraid. I have heard the boy crying." When Hagar looked up, she saw a well. She rushed over to it and brought Ishmael water. God stayed with Ishmael as he grew up. He was the ancestor of the Ishmaelites, or Arab peoples.

# Abraham and Isaac

God wanted to test Abraham's obedience, so he commanded him to take his son Isaac to the hills of Moriah and kill him.

The next morning, with great sadness in his heart, Abraham took some wood and his donkey and set out. Abraham, Isaac, and two servants traveled for three days before Abraham saw the hills of Moriah in the distance. The servants looked after the donkey while Abraham and Isaac went to pray. Isaac carried the wood, while Abraham carried the knife. Isaac asked his father where the lamb was that they were going to roast on the fire as an offering to God, but Abraham just replied that God would provide the lamb.

When they reached the right place Abraham built a stone altar, arranged the wood on it, and then tied up his son on the altar. Abraham took the long knife and raised it above his head, ready to kill his son. He was not doing this because he wanted to kill his son—far from it; he dearly loved Isaac, who was the only son he and his wife Sarah were able to have. But Abraham knew he had to obey God. Just as God had given him Isaac, so God could take him away.

Abraham was about to plunge the knife into Isaac when a voice called, "Abraham! Abraham! Do not lay your hand on the boy. Do not do anything to him. For now I know that you fear God, because you are ready to sacrifice your own son for God."

With great happiness Abraham heard God's command. He looked up and saw a ram caught in the branches of a small bush and sacrificed it to God.

*AN ISRAELITE BURIAL*
*Bodies were washed, wrapped in cloth, and usually buried in a tomb within twenty-four hours of death.*

*The body was carried to burial by friends of the dead person.*

*THINGS USED IN ANIMAL SACRIFICES*

*A knife*

*A rope*

A stone figure of a Mesopotamian man carrying a sacrificial lamb. Abraham came from Ur in Mesopotamia.

Israelites of later generations worshiped in the hills of Moriah where Abraham's act of faith took place. Solomon built the first temple there, about a thousand years later (around 950 B.C.E.). The scene below shows the temple and the city of Jerusalem at the time of Solomon.

Only the wealthy could afford to buy land for tombs, such as the underground cave where Abraham's wife Sarah was buried.

Underground tomb

Stairs

Stone door

The first chamber

The burial chamber

An urn to hold the animal's ashes.

Rams (left) and goats were sacrificed.

21

# The Marriage of Isaac and Rebekah

Abraham lived to be very old and knew that he would soon die. Isaac, his son, now a grown man, was still unmarried. Abraham wanted Isaac to marry a woman from Haran, his old home in the north. So he instructed his servant to go in search of a woman from his ancient clan who might be a suitable wife for Isaac.

His servant selected ten of his master's camels for the journey, and various precious gifts, before setting off. He came to a town and made the camels kneel down by a well. It was nearly evening, the time when the women of the town came out to fetch water from the well. Abraham's servant prayed to God for a sign. He asked God to show him the woman he had chosen by having her give water to his camels without being asked.

Before Abraham's servant had finished praying, a woman named Rebekah went down to the well to fill her jar with water. The servant hurried to meet her and asked her for a drink. She gladly offered him the jar of water that she had just filled at the well. She then drew water for his camels without being asked for it.

The servant took out a gold nose ring and two gold bracelets and presented them to Rebekah. When he found out who Rebekah's father was, the servant was glad. He realized that he had found Abraham's relatives: Rebekah was the granddaughter of Abraham's brother, Nahor. The servant placed the ring in Rebekah's nose and

*The women of the family, including the older, unmarried girls, collected water every day from a well. The water was drawn from the well by dropping a leather bucket attached to a rope into the water. It was then pulled up by hand.*

the bracelets on her wrists and they went off to greet her family.

When Rebekah's father and her brother Laban heard the story, and all about Abraham's life since he had left Haran, they were overjoyed. They permitted the servant to take Rebekah away to become Isaac's wife. Abraham's servant brought out all his master's valuable gifts and gave them to Rebekah's family, and they celebrated well into the night.

The next morning Abraham's servant and his men, and Rebekah and her maids set off on their camels to meet Isaac. They traveled a long way, and had nearly reached Abraham's homestead when Rebekah looked up from her camel and saw a man coming to meet them. She asked the servant who he was. "He is my master, Isaac," the servant replied. She modestly covered herself with her veil and went to Isaac's camp to be married.

*A wedding celebration. Every man had to marry. The marriage was usually arranged by parents when their children were still quite young. Sometimes the bride and groom were only eleven or twelve years old. It was quite common for cousins to marry.*

*Nose rings were special tokens of marriage. Both men and women wore nose rings, rings, bracelets, and earrings. Most jewelry at this time was made out of gold, silver, or bronze and was very simple in design.*

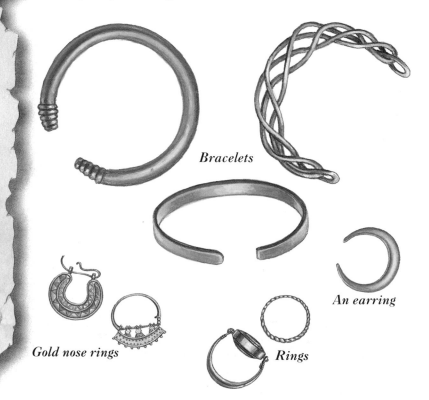

*Bracelets*

*An earring*

*Gold nose rings*

*Rings*

23

# Jacob and Esau

Isaac was forty years old when he married Rebekah. Soon after their marriage, Rebekah had twin boys. The first twin was named Esau, which means "hairy," and the second twin was named Jacob, which means "grasper of the heel," or "cheat," because he came into the world hanging onto Esau.

The boys grew up and Esau became a hunter who liked the outdoor life. Jacob was a quieter man and preferred to stay at home among the tents.

One day Esau came home from hunting to find Jacob cooking some red lentil stew. "I'm starving," he said to

*The Nubian ibex (below right) is a type of wild mountain goat that was hunted for its delicious meat. The Arabian oryx (below left) was also hunted.*

*Jars like these were used to store flour, cooking oil, lentils, and other foods and to keep them safe from blowing sand. The jars were also used to serve food at meal times.*

Jacob. "Give me some of that red stew." Jacob replied that Esau should first sell him his inheritance and then he could have the stew. "Look, I am about to die of starvation!" replied Esau. He then thought to himself, What is the use of this inheritance anyway; I want something to eat now, and he agreed to give his inheritance to Jacob in exchange for the stew.

Isaac was now a very old man and almost entirely blind. He called Esau, whom he loved more than Jacob, and asked him if he would go out and hunt

The fallow deer (left) would have been one of the animals hunted by Esau. The gazelle (below) represented grace and beauty to biblical peoples.

too blind to see the difference between his sons, but he still had his sense of touch. "Come closer," he said. He felt Jacob's hands and thought, The voice is Jacob's but the hands feel like Esau's.

After his meal Isaac said, "Come here Esau, and kiss me." When Isaac smelled his clothes, he felt sure that this was Esau and said, "May God give you Heaven's dew and Earth's richness, and you will be a blessing to the world."

No sooner had Isaac finished blessing Jacob than Esau returned and realized he had been tricked. He threatened to kill Jacob, saying, "That brother of mine has cheated me again!" But Isaac also gave Esau a blessing.

some game animals for supper. "Then I will bless you before I die," Isaac told him. Isaac said that the son he blessed would rule over the other son. Esau immediately went out to hunt. Rebekah overheard this conversation and planned to trick Isaac so that Jacob, not Esau, would receive his blessing.

Rebekah told Jacob to go out to the yard and fetch two goats, which she would cook in Isaac's favorite way. She then dressed Jacob in some of Esau's best clothes and covered his hands and neck with goatskins to make Jacob's skin feel as rough and hairy as Esau's.

When Rebekah had cooked the meal, Jacob nervously went into his father's tent and sat beside him. He said, "I am Esau. I have done as you told me. Please sit up and eat some of my game so that you may give me your blessing." Now Isaac was suspicious and asked how he had hunted the animal so quickly. Jacob replied that God must have been with him this day. Isaac was

Israelite men and women wore a linen tunic underneath a wool tunic that reached from the neck to below the knees.

A girdle of leather or cloth was tied at the waist.

# Rachel and Leah

Once he had his father's blessing, Jacob went north to Abraham's old home of Haran to find a wife. After a long journey, Jacob stopped for the night. He dreamed of a stairway reaching up to heaven. At the top was God who said, "I am the God of Abraham, and the God of your father Isaac. I will give you and your descendants the land on which you are lying." When Jacob woke up he built a pillar of stone and anointed it with oil to show that this was a special place. He named the place Bethel, which means "House of God."

Jacob continued on his journey and eventually arrived at a field where he saw a shepherdess named Rachel at a well. As the two talked they discovered that they were related: Rachel's father was Jacob's uncle Laban, his mother's brother.

Jacob stayed and worked for Laban. One day he told Laban that he loved Rachel and offered to work for seven years to earn her hand in marriage. Laban agreed to this.

It was the custom, however, for the older daughter to marry before the younger. So when the wedding night arrived, Laban swapped Rachel for Leah, his older daughter. When Jacob discovered what had happened he was furious. So Laban suggested that Jacob should finish the wedding week with Leah and then he could marry Rachel too. Although this would be in return for another seven years' work, Jacob agreed.

*People usually sat around a low table on cushions, mats, or stools to eat a wedding feast. Fruits such as melons, figs, grapes, pomegranates, and olives were eaten, as were fish, meat, and bread. Figs were made into cakes. Wine was served in jars.*

**A WEDDING FEAST**
*A bride in later times (after about 600 B.C.E.) would have worn a headband of coins at her wedding.*

*The groom went with his friends to collect the bride from her house.*

Bride's house

**INSTRUMENTS PLAYED AT A WEDDING FEAST**

A drum

A flute

This chart is a family tree. It shows the most important descendants (children, grandchildren, great-grandchildren, and so on) of Terah who was descended from Noah. The family tree shows at a glance, for example, the names of Jacob's twelve sons, from whom the twelve tribes of Israel descended. Jacob's name was changed to Israel by God, and his people became known as Israelites.

## Terah

Nahor — married Hagar (handmaiden) — Abraham — married Sarah — Haran

Bethuel — Ishmael — married Rebekah — Isaac — Iscah  Milcah  Lot

Laban  Rebekah — Esau — Ammon  Moab

Leah  Rachel — married Zilpah (handmaiden) — married Leah — Jacob (Israel) — married Rachel — married Bilhah (handmaiden)

Gad, Asher

Reuben, Simeon, Levi, Judah, Issachar, Zebulun, Dinah

Joseph  Benjamin

Dan, Naphtali

Ephraim, Manasseh

Bridal couples sat under a canopy at their wedding feast, which was held at the groom's house (probably outside). Couples wore their finest clothes.

The bride and groom may have drunk from the same goblet before smashing it as a sign of their wedding vows.

Brass cymbals

A bronze sistrum, a kind of metal rattle

27

# THE ISRAELITES IN EGYPT

*Stories of a nation without a country*

*Flax*

*Cumin*

## Joseph and His Brothers

Jacob's wives bore him many sons, but one of them, named Joseph, was his favorite child because he was born to Rachel and Jacob in their old age. Jacob decided to weave Joseph a beautiful coat.

One night Joseph dreamed that the sun, moon, and eleven stars bowed down to him. When he told his family about the dream they were furious. They thought the dream was meant to tell the future: the sun and the moon were Joseph's father and mother, and

the stars were his eleven brothers. Jacob said to him sternly, "Do you think we are all going to come and bow down to you?" Joseph's brothers were already jealous. Now they were so angry they began to plot against him.

One day Jacob sent Joseph to the fields where his brothers were grazing sheep. When Joseph's brothers saw him alone without his father to protect him,

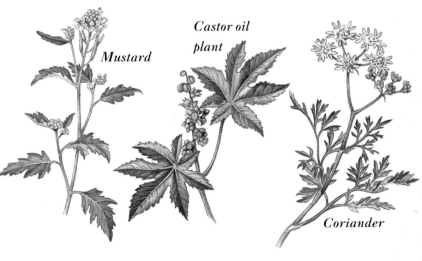

*Mustard*

*Castor oil plant*

*Coriander*

*Cumin, coriander, and mustard are some of the kinds of spices that were carried by traders in biblical times. They also traded oils, such as castor oil, and linen—a type of cloth made of fibers taken from the flax plant.*

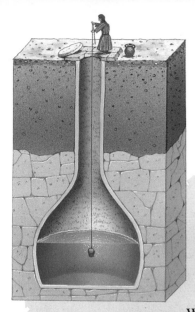

*A cistern was a small reservoir for storing rainwater. It was dug deep in the ground to stop the water from evaporating in the sun.*

they decided that this was their chance for revenge. "Let's kill him and throw him into this cistern. We can say that a wild animal got him."

But Reuben, one of the brothers told them not to spill the blood of their own family. When Joseph reached them they took off his special coat, and threw him into the dry cistern. Laughing at their young brother, they sat down to eat.

After Reuben had left, the brothers saw a camel caravan of Ishmaelites coming toward them. Ishmaelites were traders who came from the family of Ishmael, Abraham's first son. Another of the brothers,

named Judah, thought of selling Joseph to the traders who were taking spices to Egypt. They pulled Joseph out of the cistern and sold him to the Ishmaelites for twenty shekels. The average price for a slave was thirty shekels (about $30 today) so Joseph was a bargain. Then they stained his coat with the blood of a dead goat to make it look as though Joseph had been attacked by a wild animal.

They took the coat back to their father. Jacob recognized it immediately and threw up his hands in horror. "My son's coat—he has been devoured by an animal!" Jacob mourned Joseph for a long time and refused to be comforted by his other sons and daughter.

*Shekels*

*Camel caravans traveled along trade routes between the north and Egypt. They carried important spices used in cooking food and making perfume. There were many traders in this area buying and selling silver, iron, tin, lead, slaves, bronze, ivory, and horses.*

# Joseph and the Great Famine

When the Ishmaelites arrived in Egypt they sold Joseph to Potiphar, the captain of the Pharaoh's army. Potiphar liked Joseph and appointed him to look after his house. But Potiphar's wife told her husband that Joseph had tried to attack her. Potiphar was enraged and threw Joseph into the Pharaoh's prison. At this time people were put in prison to stop them from leaving, as well as to punish them for a crime.

Once again Joseph was a prisoner. But he could still tell the future by interpreting dreams. He correctly predicted that one of the prisoners would be restored to his place as the Pharaoh's servant. Some time later, when the Pharaoh was having trouble understanding a dream, the servant remembered Joseph and told the Pharaoh. The Pharaoh called him out of prison. "In my dream," related the Pharaoh, "I was standing on the bank of the Nile River and seven fat cows came out of the river. They were followed by seven thin, scrawny cows who ate the fat ones, and yet looked no fatter afterward."

Joseph explained that the seven fat cows were seven years of good harvest when the Egyptians would have lots of food. But then seven years of famine would follow. Joseph said this was God's way of warning the Pharaoh of the coming disaster and advised the Pharaoh to start storing grain for the bad years.

The Pharaoh accepted Joseph's wise words and made him an important official, known as a vizier. Joseph was given gold rings, necklaces, and fine robes. He married the daughter of the Egyptian priest of Heliopolis. When he was thirty years old Joseph began to oversee the collection and storage of grain from the fields by the Nile River.

*An Egyptian vizier was one of the highest officials in the land. He would have worn expensive clothes and jewels to show his status. Wigs made of human hair were worn by rich Egyptians. The wigs were stuck on with beeswax.*

*A scene from an Egyptian wall painting showing herdsmen counting their cows and bulls. The animals were regularly inspected and their numbers recorded.*

*A model wooden granary that was found inside an Egyptian tomb. It shows a scribe recording the amount of grain before it is stored in three large bins. In the foreground a woman is grinding barley on a stone.*

After seven years the harvests started to fail and people from every part of Egypt began coming to Joseph for the grain he had saved. But as each year passed the famine grew worse, and people flooded into Egypt from all the surrounding countries.

One day, as Joseph was giving grain to some foreigners, he recognized his brothers in the crowd. Jacob must have sent them because of the famine at home. They did not recognize Joseph,

so he pretended not to know them. Joseph spoke sternly to them and accused them of spying. In fear, they said they weren't spies, just twelve brothers; one had died, and the youngest stayed behind in Canaan. Joseph ordered them to fetch this brother, as only then would he believe them. They quickly returned with their youngest brother, Benjamin, who was the only other child of Joseph's mother. They gave Joseph gifts and bowed down before him.

Joseph could not keep his secret any longer. He ordered all the Egyptian officials out of the room and said to his brothers, "I am your brother Joseph whom you sold into slavery." They were terrified of what he would do but Joseph still loved his brothers and forgave them. He told them to return to Canaan and bring their father Jacob and their families back to Egypt to live.

Joseph went out in his chariot to meet them when they returned. The moment Jacob saw his long-lost son he wept with joy. Joseph took his family to a fertile area by the Nile called Goshen, where the Israelites settled.

*Barley and wheat were grown in ancient Egypt.*

Wheat

Barley

31

# The Pharaoh's Slaves

Three hundred years after the death of Joseph, the Israelites still lived in the land of Goshen in Egypt. However, times had changed, and a new dynasty of pharaohs had forgotten the days when Joseph saved the country from starvation.

The new Pharaoh planned to construct many new buildings. He wanted to build a grand palace for himself and huge grain stores in case there was another famine as in the time of Joseph. He also wanted to control the growing number of Israelites, so he made them his slaves.

The Pharaoh's slave masters treated the Israelites very harshly. Many of the Israelites had to work in the fields during the hottest part of the day or to make and haul bricks to build the Pharaoh's city.

Still the Pharaoh feared that the Israelites might gain power. So he said to the Israelite midwives, "When you help an

**MAKING BRICKS**
*Mud was collected from the banks of the Nile River.*

*Straw and water were added to the mud. The straw made the mixture stronger.*

*Slaves transported the mixture to the molding and drying area.*

*An inkwell and reed pens*

*The black ink in this inkwell was made from soot.*

Israelite woman to have a baby, take note whether it is a boy or a girl: if it is a boy, kill him, if it is a girl, let her live." The midwives were afraid of the Pharaoh, but they feared God more. So they disobeyed the Pharaoh and pretended that all the Israelite children were born before they could get there. When the Pharaoh realized what was happening he ordered all his people to throw every new-born Israelite boy into the river.

The tombs and palaces of the pharaohs often had walls decorated with stories told in Egyptian writing. The writing above tells the story of a hunt. Writing was invented in Babylonia, near where Abraham was born, but long before his time. The idea of writing then came to Egypt. The Egyptians made up their own language of picture signs known as hieroglyphs. People wrote on tablets of clay or with a reed pen on papyrus paper.

*A reed pen*

Nearly everybody in Egypt worked for the Pharaoh. These slaves are building part of a temple complex. Some people worked as builders, others as miners or stone quarriers. Yet others repaired the canals and fences that were damaged when the Nile River burst its banks each year.

*Papyrus reeds*

*The bricks were left out in the sun to dry.*

*A slave carried the dried bricks to the building site using a sling attached to a yoke.*

*A papyrus scroll rolled around wood. "Paper" was made from papyrus reeds.*

# Moses and the Burning Bush

During the time of the Pharaoh's order that all male Israelite children should be thrown into the river, a husband and wife from the family of Levi (who had descended from one of Jacob's sons) hid their baby boy for three months. The time came when they could not hide him any longer, so they put him in a waterproof basket and placed it in the reeds of the Nile River.

The baby's sister hid there to see what would happen. The Pharaoh's daughter spotted the child and felt sorry for him. His sister came out of hiding and offered to find a woman from the Israelites to nurse him. The Pharaoh's daughter agreed, and the girl returned with the child's mother. The Pharaoh's

*An ancient Egyptian board game known as senet. It was made of ivory and ebony and belonged to a pharaoh.*

*Papyrus reeds were used to make many things, including baskets and mats. The basket that Moses was found in would probably have been shaped like a boat.*

daughter told her to nurse the baby, without realizing that she was his real mother. When the child was older he was taken to the Pharaoh's daughter, who named him Moses, which means "drawn out of the water." Moses was brought up in the Egyptian palace.

When Moses was a grown man he saw the suffering of the Israelites, his own people, as they worked every day for the Pharaoh. One day Moses saw an Egyptian beating an Israelite, and in his rage he killed the Egyptian and hid his body in the sand.

Word soon got around that Moses had murdered an Egyptian, and he fled to the land of Midian. As he sat down by a well after his journey, seven daughters of a Midianite priest came along to give water to their sheep. Some local shepherds started bothering the girls

A toy cat or lion

A spinning top made of quartz

A wooden toy horse

A doll with wool for hair

closer. "Moses, Moses," cried out a voice. "Do not come any closer, but take off your sandals for this is holy ground." Moses quickly took them off and then hid his face in fear.

God spoke from the bush. "I am the God of Abraham, Isaac, and Jacob. I have seen the misery of my people in Egypt who are slaves of the Pharaoh. I will rescue them, and take them to a land flowing with milk and honey. Now, go. I am sending you to the Pharaoh to save my people the Israelites."

But Moses was terrified of God's task. He argued that he was not strong or clever enough to fight the Pharaoh. "Please send someone else," begged Moses. God said he would enable him to perform miracles with his staff and would send his brother Aaron to help him. Moses had to do as God wished and so he set off for Egypt.

and tried to drive their sheep away. Moses came to their rescue and the shepherds left. The girls were so grateful they took Moses back to meet their father, Jethro. Moses stayed for forty years, married one of the priest's daughters, Zipporah, and had two sons.

All the time Moses was in Midian he remembered his people enslaved in Egypt. One day while Moses was out looking after Jethro's flock, he came to Mount Horeb, the holy mountain. A bush on the far side of the desert caught his attention. As he looked harder it started to burn and Moses noticed that although the bush was on fire, it was not destroyed. Moses walked

This Egyptian wand is similar to the staff God gave Moses. It is made of ivory and is decorated with pictures of animals and Egyptian goddesses. These wands were used by Egyptians to draw a circle around their beds at night. It was thought that this would protect the sleeper from snakes and scorpions.

# The Plagues

After God commanded Moses to free the Israelites, Moses and his brother Aaron traveled to Egypt. At their meeting with the Pharaoh, Aaron's miracle staff turned into a snake as a sign of the power of God. But the Pharaoh's magicians did the same trick. The Pharaoh would need to see more miracles to believe in God.

When Moses and Aaron next went to see the Pharaoh, Aaron touched the Nile with his staff. Immediately the river turned to blood. All the fish died, and the river smelled so bad that the Egyptians could not drink the water.

This miracle may refer to the fact that when the Nile floods, deposits of mud turn the river a reddish-brown color. This looks like blood, and the water may be undrinkable as in the story. But this plague did not work because the

Pharaoh did not care that his people had no water to drink.

Seven days later, Aaron stretched his staff over Egypt's canals and ponds. Masses of frogs started to leap onto the land. They jumped into people's homes and into the Pharaoh's palace. Frogs were everywhere, even in the bedroom of the Pharaoh's daughter. This upset the Pharaoh, and he begged Moses to take them away. But when God killed all the frogs, the Pharaoh went back on his promise to let the Israelites leave.

God brought more plagues on the Egyptians. He turned the soil into gnats which attacked people and animals. Swarms of flies then flew into the Pharaoh's palace. God diseased all the cattle, and then sent a plague of boils to cover the skin of the Egyptians and their animals. The Pharaoh was still stubborn, and so God sent three more plagues on him.

A terrible hailstorm destroyed the animals and the crops in the fields. Then swarms of locusts covered the land and ate what little was left after the hail. Finally, the whole land became completely dark for three days. But God left light where the Israelites lived so that the Pharaoh could see that he had chosen them as his people.

The Pharaoh begged Moses to tell God to end each new plague. Each time the Pharaoh promised to let

*A small stela, or gravestone, showing the figure of the Egyptian god Horus, standing on crocodiles. He is holding snakes, scorpions, and gazelles in his hands. The stela was thought to have magical powers to protect people against these "evil" creatures. The Egyptians believed in magic, and there are many tales of famous Egyptian magicians, such as the Pharaoh's magicians in this story.*

the Israelites go once the plague had ended. But the Pharaoh always forgot his promise and forbade them to leave.

God decided to send one last plague to Egypt. Moses told the Israelites how to prepare, in order to avoid the final plague. On the evening before the last plague, every Israelite family killed a young lamb and roasted it over the fire. Using bunches of hyssop they painted the lambs' blood on the doors of their houses to show that they were Israelites and not Egyptians. They then ate their meal of lamb and flat, unleavened bread and waited inside until morning.

At midnight an angel sent by God went through the land killing all the eldest children of Egypt. The angel avoided the doors of houses marked with blood. He knew they were the houses of the Israelites and passed over them. Loud crying and screaming filled the night air because the first-born child of every family except the Israelites had died. Even the first-born cattle had died.

The Pharaoh called Moses and said, "Up! Leave my people. Go from this land of Egypt." So the Israelites left the land where they had been slaves for so many years.

The meal the Israelites ate on their last night in Egypt is called the Passover because God passed over their houses and saved their children.

*The plant hyssop was a type of herb that grew in the region. The Israelites used bunches of hyssop to brush their doors with the blood of a lamb as a sign to the angel.*

*The Israelites lived separately from the Egyptians and other peoples in cramped, single-story houses. The houses were built of bricks made from mud, collected by the Israelites from the Nile delta—the area of land formed by mud where the Nile River reaches the sea. Their homes were situated in Goshen, not far from the Nile delta.*

# The Exodus

On the night of the Passover, the Israelites were driven out of Egypt by the angry Pharaoh. Their journey is known as the Exodus. They were in such a hurry they did not have time to bake their bread and had to take the dough and yeast in troughs on their shoulders. About half a million families left Egypt with their cattle, sheep, and goats. They traveled from Rameses to Succoth without stopping. By day God led them with a pillar of cloud, by night with a pillar of fire.

Eventually they came to the sea and camped because they thought that they were safe from the Pharaoh. But when the Pharaoh heard that the Israelites had fled, he changed his mind. He no longer had an army of slaves. "After them, you fools!" he barked out at his officers. "Do not let the Israelites get away."

The Pharaoh's cavalry rushed off in pursuit of the Israelites and quickly caught up. In terror, the Israelites saw the Egyptians on the horizon. They cried out to Moses, "Have you brought us into the desert to die? Better to be a slave in Egypt than dead in the desert!" "Don't be afraid," Moses replied, confident that God would save them.

Moses stretched out his staff across the sea in front of him and God held back the water, allowing the Israelites to cross. But when the Pharaoh's army tried to cross, his chariots swerved on the mud. Some soldiers tried to turn back, afraid that the sea was about to crush them to death.

*FOOD IN THE DESERT*
*God provided the Israelites with manna, which may have been the sweet drops of fluid secreted by insects living on tamarisk trees. The drops fell to the ground and were then collected.*

*Quails were eaten when they fell from the sky exhausted by the heat.*

*An oasis was the only source of water in the desert.*

*HUNTING WEAPONS*

*A spear*

*A knife was an essential tool and weapon.*

38

Moses stretched his staff out over the sea again, and the water rolled back into place like a huge tidal wave. All of the Egyptians were drowned. The Israelites, safe on the other side of the sea, looked back in amazement at their escape.

After they had fled from Egypt, the Israelites wandered in the deserts of Sinai for forty years.

A map showing the probable route of the Exodus. It is thought that the sea the Israelites crossed may have been an area of marshy land called the "Reed Sea," between the Gulf of Suez and the Mediterranean Sea. The Israelites then camped in the desert for forty years before invading Canaan, the Promised Land, from the east. Earlier, some Israelites had disobeyed Moses and attempted to invade Canaan from the south. They were defeated and sadly returned to the desert.

The chariot was the most important part of the Egyptian army. Chariots were perfect for chasing the enemies of the Pharaoh and also for long-distance marches and wars.

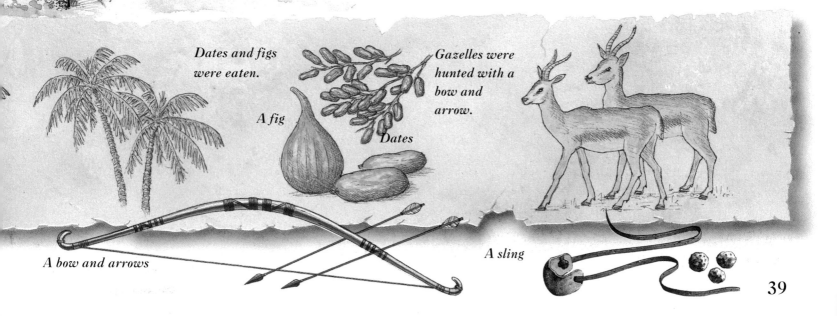

Dates and figs were eaten.

A fig

Dates

Gazelles were hunted with a bow and arrow.

A bow and arrows

A sling

# THE PROMISED LAND

*Stories of how a people found their homeland*

## Moses and the Ten Commandments

Three months after their escape from Egypt, the Israelites arrived at the Sinai desert and made camp at the foot of Mount Sinai. They were tired after their long journey and concerned about their dwindling food stores. When no food at all could be found God provided them with manna to eat, which they collected from the ground after the dew.

Moses and the Israelites were scared. God had called from the mountain, commanding Moses to speak to him. He told Moses that he would appear in three days' time and that the Israelites should pray, wash their clothes, and on no account set foot on the mountain.

On the third day thunder roared and everyone in the camp rushed to Mount Sinai to receive God's law.

Moses climbed up the mountain. The Israelites waited for six days and then God spoke his commandments: "I am the Lord your God, who brought you out of Egypt.

"You shall have no other gods but me.

"You shall not make a false god out of anything on the earth or in the sea. I am a jealous God and will punish those who hate me.

"Do not use my name in vain.

"Remember the Sabbath day and keep it holy. Work for six days, but not on the

*The Israelites spoke Hebrew. This is a fragment of Phoenician script which was very much like the Hebrew script. The writing on the stone tablets given to Moses may have looked something like this.*

seventh because God made Heaven and Earth in six days and rested on the seventh day.

"Do as your father and mother tell you.

"You shall not kill anyone.

"You shall not take another man's wife, or another woman's husband.

"You shall not steal.

"You shall not lie about your neighbor.

"You shall not want anything that is your neighbor's."

Moses stayed on the mountain for forty days. While he was there, the Israelites asked Aaron, the priest, to make them a new god. They gave Aaron their gold Egyptian earrings which he melted in a fire to form a single block of gold in the shape of a calf. The Israelites worshiped the idol.

Moses returned from Mount Sinai with the ten commandments written on two stone tablets. When he saw the Israelites praising the idol he smashed the tablets. The next day Moses climbed the mountain to plead forgiveness for the Israelites. He returned with new tablets as a record of God's laws.

| ARAMAIC (ELEPHANTINE) | HEBREW CURSIVE | MODERN ROMAN |
|---|---|---|
| ✗ | ✗ | A |
| 7 | 9 | B |
| ∧ | ∧ | C |
| ⤳ | ⤳ | D |
| ∧ | ⅄ | E |
| ⅂ | ⅄ | F |
| ┐ | ⇌ | Z |
| ⊓ | ⊓ | H |
| ⊍ | ⊂ | |
| ⅃ | ⅄ | I |
| ⅄ | ⅄ | K |
| ⅃ | ⅃ | L |
| ⅄ | ⅄ | M |
| ⅃ | ⅄ | N |
| ⅃ | ⅄ | |
| ⌄ | ⌀ | O |
| ⅃ | ⅄ | P |
| ⌐ | ⌐ | |
| ⌐ | ⅄ | Q |
| ⅄ | ⅄ | R |
| ⌄ | ⌄ | S |
| ⅃ | ✗ | T |

*Along with the ten commandments, God gave the Israelites instructions on how to worship. They had to construct a tent, called a tabernacle, as a meeting place. The tent was made of layers of animal skins covering a wooden frame. It was hung with curtains of finely woven linen. The holy stone tablets were kept in a gold-covered wooden chest known as the ark.*

# The Fall of Jericho

*A ram's horn*

The Israelites wandered in the desert for forty years before they found Canaan, the Promised Land. Moses climbed up a high mountain, called Mount Nebo, and saw the land, but he never entered it. Then, at the age of one hundred and twenty, Moses died, and was buried on the mountain.

A man named Joshua now became the leader of the Israelites. The people of Canaan did not follow God's laws, and Joshua was determined to take this land which God meant for the Israelites. So he sent two men into Canaan as spies. They stayed in the house of a woman named Rahab in the city of Jericho. When the king of Jericho heard about the spies he sent soldiers after them.

Rahab hid the spies on the roof and told the soldiers that the men had left the city. The spies escaped by rope over the walls of Jericho.

Joshua then led his soldiers against the city of Jericho. The soldiers were followed by seven priests carrying the ark, the wooden chest that held the stone tablets of Moses. The Israelites believed that as long as they carried the ark with them, God would be on their side.

The twelve tribes of Israel marched around Jericho for seven days. On the seventh day the priests blasted on their horns, the

## WORSHIPING IN THE TABERNACLE

*It was only after God told Moses how his people were to praise him that the Israelites had a formal system of worship.*

*The priests would sacrifice an animal, sprinkle its blood on the altar, and wash it in the basin. It was then burned.*

*The altar used to burn offerings*

*Washing basin, or laver*

*Altar for burning incense*

Israelites began to shout, and the walls of Jericho started to crumble. The Israelites rushed in through the gaps in the walls, set all the houses on fire and killed everyone in the city. Only Rahab and her family were spared. The ark was then carried into the city as the Israelites celebrated their first victory over the people of Canaan.

*Before they conquered Jericho, the Israelites fought battles with the peoples who lived east of the Jordan River. Some of their land was captured by the Israelites and became part of the territory divided up among the twelve tribes of Israel.*

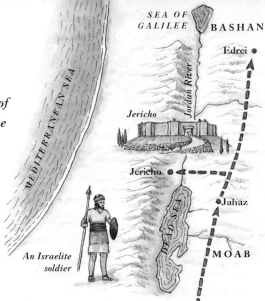

*An Israelite soldier*

*The Israelites invaded Canaan from the east. After they crossed the Jordan River they came to Jericho (left). Jericho is perhaps the oldest city in the world, in existence since before 6000 B.C.E.*

*Inside the tabernacle were the altar for burning incense, the table for showbread, and the menorah. The table held twelve loaves of flat, unleavened showbread (one for each of the tribes of Israel).*

*Only the priests were allowed to see the ark of the covenant. Carved cherubim sat on top of the ark to guard the stone tablets inside.*

*Incense holder or censer*

*A menorah or seven-branched lampstand*

*Ark of the covenant*

# Deborah the Prophetess

After the fall of Jericho, the Israelites captured one city after another in Canaan. They divided their army into groups: some went to conquer cities in the south and others went north. The Canaanite kings were afraid of these new people of God—how could they be defeated when they were helped by God himself?

It was not long before the Israelites had conquered nearly all of Canaan. They divided the land (known as Israel) among themselves so that each tribe had its own territory, except the Levites whom God had made a tribe of priests. It was the Levites' job to take care of Israel's religious life. Israel would only continue to receive God's blessing if the Israelites obeyed the ten

*The Levite priests wore white robes with a sash tied at the waist. They performed the religious duties at the tabernacle. The priests were also teachers and judged disputes.*

commandments given to Moses by God on Mount Sinai.

But the Israelites did not always keep God's laws. Time and time again they disobeyed God and had to ask him for forgiveness. Some even followed the evil ways of the Canaanites.

One particularly cruel Canaanite king, named Jabin, ruled the Israelites for twenty years. Israel did not have its own king, but was ruled by a warrior, who led them into battle and also acted as a judge whenever there were arguments between people or tribes.

One of these judges was named Deborah. The Israelites came to the place

*On a Canaanite chariot, one man held the reins of the horses while the other shot arrows at the enemy. A quiver for the arrows was fitted to the side of the chariot. Infantrymen followed on foot carrying shields and sickle-shaped swords.*

The Israelites were no longer wandering nomads. They gave up their tents and built their own homes. They became a nation of farmers, growing fruit and vegetables. Most Israelites had to settle in the mountains because they could not drive out the Canaanites who lived in the valleys.

where she sat, called Deborah's palm, and asked her guidance on an emergency in the northern part of the land. King Jabin had taken control of all the Israelites' trade routes and was threatening to massacre the northern tribes of Israel. Deborah sent for her commander, Barak, and told him of a vision she had received from God: Barak was going to defeat Jabin's great army of thousands of soldiers and nine hundred iron chariots with just ten thousand men. Barak was nervous, but he agreed to follow Deborah's advice.

Barak and Deborah went to the top of Mount Tabor with their army of ten thousand foot soldiers and camped. Here, on high ground, they were safer from attack. When the time was right, Deborah gave the signal, and Barak and his men charged down the hillside. It suddenly started to pour with rain, which was unusual for this region, and the river at the bottom of the

mountain began to flood. Its banks overflowed and turned the battlefield to mud. The wheels of King Jabin's chariots stuck in the mud. The Israelites charged at them, brandishing their swords and farming tools such as axes and sickles.

Jabin's army was slaughtered, though its commander, Sisera, escaped. Seeking shelter in a nearby village, he was let into one house. The people who lived there said they would keep watch over him. But when Sisera was asleep, the woman of the house took a tent peg and hammered it through his head and into the ground below.

*Deborah's palm would have been a date palm, a tall tree with six-foot leaves.*

45

# Samson in the Temple

About fifty years after the death of Deborah, a new enemy, the Philistines, arose against the Israelites. They were also known as the "sea peoples" because they lived by the Mediterranean Sea in Philistia. They were a powerful nation, with weapons made of iron, and they defeated the Israelites in battle for many years.

One day a woman from the tribe of Dan gave birth to a special boy. An angel had appeared to the woman saying that her son would grow up to lead the Israelites to victory against the Philistines. This was on condition that he never cut his hair. The child was known as a Nazirite—someone who belongs to God.

The boy was named Samson, and he grew up to be very strong.

*A Philistine warrior*

*An Israelite warrior*

*Both the Israelite and Philistine warriors wore simple garments of shirts and kilts.*

He could win a fight against the Philistines single-handedly. Once he killed a thousand Philistines, using only the jawbone of a donkey.

Samson spent a lot of time in Philistine country. There he met and fell in love with a woman named Delilah. The Philistines

*This is a Philistine warship. The Philistines, or sea peoples, were once pirates who sailed around the coasts of the Mediterranean. By Samson's time, they had become the main enemies of the Israelites.*

*A reconstruction of a Philistine temple from Tell Qasile in northern Philistia. It is smaller than the one Samson destroyed. The main hall had pillars of cedarwood and seats around the walls. A statue of the Philistine god would have stood on the raised platform in the corner. The roof was supported by wooden beams.*

promised to pay Delilah eleven hundred shekels of silver to discover the secret of Samson's strength. At first Samson refused to reveal his secret, then he finally gave in and told Delilah, "If my head were shaved, my strength would leave me."

Delilah whispered to one of the house guards to bring a razor and cut off Samson's hair while he slept. After his head was completely shaved, she shouted "Samson, the

*The Philistines are thought to have come originally from the Mycenaean culture of south and central Greece. This is a Mycenaean jug, an amphora, from about 1400 B.C.E, decorated with a drawing of an octopus.*

Philistines are attacking!" He jumped up and ran out to fight, but all of his strength had gone. The Philistines grabbed him, gouged out his eyes, and put him in prison.

Some time later, the Philistines were in the temple of Dagon worshiping their god when they asked for Samson to be brought in for their amusement. By this time, Samson's hair had grown back, and he prayed to God that his strength would also be restored, just this once.

When the Philistines brought him out, he stood between two pillars of the temple, gathered his strength, and pushed with all his might. The pillars gave way and the roof came crashing down, burying all the Philistines—and Samson—alive. Samson died trying to destroy the Philistines so that the Israelites could live in freedom.

# The Story of Ruth

**D**uring the time of the judges, famine spread across Judah in southern Israel. To escape their hunger, Elimelech, his wife Naomi, and their two sons moved from their home in Bethlehem to Moab, a place east of the Dead Sea.

Not long after arriving, Elimelech died. In time, his sons married Orpah and Ruth, two women from Moab. But after ten years, tragedy struck—Naomi's two sons died. Since Naomi had lost both her husband and her sons, she decided to return to her relatives in Bethlehem. She told Orpah and Ruth to stay in Moab and go back to their mothers' houses. Orpah agreed, but Ruth said she would go to Bethlehem with Naomi.

Naomi and Ruth returned to Bethlehem during the barley harvest. Ruth went out into the fields and joined the workwomen gathering the barley. The fields were owned by Boaz, a wealthy relative of Naomi and Elimelech. Boaz was kind to Ruth, knowing that she was a widow and a stranger in a foreign land.

Naomi told Ruth to make herself look beautiful and go to the place where Boaz was working. "Don't let him recognize

*HARVESTING*
*Reapers in the fields cut off the tops of the barley with sickles. Women picked up the barley left by the cutters. This was known as "gleaning."*

*The sheaves of barley were heaped into a basket, and pressed down by two men using a long rod.*

*TOOLS FOR FARMING*

*An Egyptian sickle with flint cutting edge*

*A mattock, a type of hoe*

*An iron-bladed sickle from 1000 B.C.E.*

*A diagram of the Israelites' farming year. It shows at what time of year different agricultural activities took place. We can see: plowing the land (1), sowing the seed (2), growing the crops (3), harvesting: citrus fruits (4), flax (5), barley (6), wheat (7), grapes (8), olives (9), dates (10), and storing the produce (11).*

you while he is eating and drinking. But when he lies down, go and carefully turn back the covering at his feet and lie down yourself."

Ruth followed Naomi's instructions, and during the night Boaz woke up to discover that there was a woman lying at his feet. Ruth told Boaz who she was and asked him to spread his cloak over her as a sign that he would marry her. But Boaz said there was another man who, as a closer relative, had the first choice of her because, when a woman's husband died, it was the custom for the husband's brother or nearest relative to marry the widow.

The next morning Boaz offered Ruth to the closer relative. To show that he was not interested, the man offered Boaz his sandal, a sign that he was passing the opportunity to Boaz. Boaz received Ruth with open arms because she had stayed loyal to Naomi and had been brave enough to come to a foreign land. In time, Ruth gave birth to a boy named Obed, who grew up to be the father of Jesse and the grandfather of David, Israel's greatest king.

*Oxen dragged a threshing sledge. It had flints fixed along its underside to cut up the straw and separate it from the grain.*

*The farmer used a large wooden fork called a winnowing fan to throw the separated grain and straw into the air. The straw was blown away by the wind and the grain collected with a shovel.*

*A wooden shovel*

*A winnowing fan*

# DAVID'S KINGDOM

*Stories of how a nation was built*

*David's sling*

# David and Goliath

*Slingstones*

The time of the judges' rule had ended. Now the Israelites needed a strong king to unite them and make them victorious in battle.

The Israelites made Saul their king. Though Saul united the tribes in battle and built the Israelite army, he disobeyed God. So God told his prophet Samuel to go to Jesse, a man who lived in Bethlehem, because, "I have chosen one of his sons to be king." When Samuel arrived in Bethlehem, the town elders told Jesse to fetch his eight sons. It was the youngest son, the shepherd boy David, whom God told Samuel was his choice. David became a musician and page in Saul's court.

The Israelites and the Philistines were fighting at this time. In one battle the Philistines lined up on a hill and the Israelites lined up on the hill on the other side of the valley. The Philistines' greatest warrior, Goliath, stepped forward and shouted to the Israelites to pick one man to fight him. Whoever won the fight would win the battle for his people.

The Israelites were terrified of Goliath who was nine feet tall and protected by heavy armor. Only David came forward. Saul, who did not know that David was chosen as his successor, said, "You are just a shepherd. You won't stand a chance!" But David replied, "When a bear attacks my sheep, I rescue the sheep from its mouth, and kill the bear. This Philistine will be like the bear who has come to attack my people." Saul thought and then said, "Go fight Goliath, and God be with you."

David took five smooth stones and a sling. When Goliath saw this boy he wondered if the Israelites had gone mad. As David moved closer to Goliath, he slung a stone and hit him in the forehead, knocking him dead. David ran up to Goliath, took his sword, and cut off his head. Now it was the Philistines who were terrified, and they fled from the Israelites.

*The higher ranking Philistine soldiers wore protective coats of mail. Mail is made of small plates of bronze hung on woolen mesh, like the tiles on the roof of a house.*

*The Israelites (below) would have been armed for battle with slings and slingstones, axes, bows and arrows, swords, and spears. The Philistines (left) had chariots and horses, whereas the Israelites had only foot soldiers. Although the Philistines usually beat the Israelites in battle, the Israelites won some important fights by using clever tactics.*

# The Capture of Jerusalem

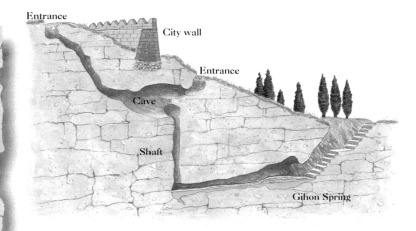

**D**avid grew up to be a clever soldier. He pretended to be a friend of the Philistines so they would send him out to fight their enemies and bring them back what he had captured. He usually defeated these enemies but he only handed over enough of their possessions to keep the Philistines satisfied. David kept the other captured goods and gave them to his soldiers, thus earning their loyalty.

In time, David built up a large army of his own. He moved his headquarters away from the Philistines to the town of Hebron, high in the hills of Judah, a kingdom in southern Israel. Abraham and his family were buried near Hebron. David became very popular with the people of Judah, who remembered how he had killed the giant Goliath and could see that he still protected them from their enemies. When Saul died in a battle, the people of Judah made

*This diagram shows how David captured the city of Jerusalem. It is most likely that David's men discovered a tunnel going into the side of the hill below the city wall which joined another tunnel running from an underground pool.*

David their king. Israel was not a united country at that time.

David was thirty years old when he became king, and he ruled Judah for seven and a half years. He was very successful and won nearly every battle he fought. The elders of Israel came to Hebron to meet him and crown him king of all Israel.

When the Philistines heard this news, and realized that David had betrayed them, they marched to attack him. David sent out scouts who saw the Philistines coming. He then

*Before David conquered Jerusalem the city was called Jebus. The inhabitants were the only Canaanites whom the Israelites had not conquered. The city was difficult to attack because it was built on top of a hill.*

commanded his troops to hide in the woods and wait. When the Philistine army passed by, the Israelites ambushed and slaughtered them all. It had been a long time since the Israelites had been able to defeat the mighty Philistines.

Now that David was king of all Israel he needed a suitable capital. Hebron was the capital town of Judah, but he needed somewhere the Israelites of the north would accept as well. There was one city, set on seven hills and held by the Jebusites, which the Israelites had never been able to capture because of its strong defensive position. It was the city of Jerusalem—it would be a perfect capital for Israel.

Jerusalem was thought to be impossible to conquer, because of its high stone walls. But David discovered a tunnel which led from a water pool outside the city under the city wall. The Jebusites used this tunnel to fetch their water. David's men scrambled along the tunnel, and climbed up into the city and captured it. They let the Jebusites live because they had surrendered without a fight.

*The stonemasons from Tyre cut out large rectangular blocks of limestone to build King David's new palace. The limestone was cut in the quarry while it was still soft because it hardens when exposed to hot, dry air.*

*The kind of harp played in Israel was small enough to carry. The harpist often played and walked at the same time. This type of harp is called a kinnor. David would have played one like this when he was a boy tending his father's sheep on the hills.*

When David's friend the king of Tyre (a port on the Mediterranean coast north of Israel) heard that David had captured Jerusalem, he sent his best carpenters and stonemasons to build him a royal palace. Everyone was excited and sang and danced through the streets. All the elders of Israel assembled to celebrate. Then they held a ceremony in which the holy ark of God was carried up to the city. David proudly led the procession, dancing in front of the ark all the way up the hill and through the gates of the city.

By bringing the ark into Jerusalem the Israelites believed that they were bringing God into their city.

# Solomon's Temple

When King David died, his son Solomon became the new king of the Israelites. Solomon had a peaceful reign because David had defeated all of Israel's many enemies.

Solomon spent his time building palaces, a fleet of ships, and even a whole city. But the most precious place of all was the one God commanded Solomon to build. It was a temple for the people of Israel to worship in. God gave Solomon detailed instructions for building the temple, and Solomon followed them exactly.

Solomon used the finest materials in the region. Wood from the cedar and cypress trees of Phoenicia was transported over a hundred miles to Jerusalem to make the roof and line the temple walls. Craftsmen laid gold in the great doors and made huge columns of bronze. The walls of the temple were made of rectangular blocks of stone.

After seven years of building, everything was finally finished. People came from all over the country to see the splendors of the new temple and to give thanks to God.

*Cypress*

*Cedar*

*The bronze sea*

*The altar*

**BUILDING THE TEMPLE**
*Logs were loaded onto Solomon's ships.*

*TOOLS FOR BUILDING*

54

*A tool for shaving wood*

*Nails*

*An adze*

A ram carved in gold. The Israelites used to offer rams to thank God for helping them. The Israelites believed that the sweet smell of roast lamb rising to heaven made God happy.

Solomon's high priest wore fine colorful robes. On his chest he wore a linen breastplate with twelve precious stones set into it. Each stone represented one of the twelve tribes of Israel that had settled in Canaan.

Basins of water on wheels were used to wash the sacrificial lambs.

A cutaway illustration of Solomon's temple. The altar was for roasting lambs. The bronze sea and the trolley basins were used for washing. Inside the temple were the candle tables, the golden table for bread, and the small altar for burning incense (used to make perfumed smoke). At the back of the temple, steps led to the Holy of Holies, where only the high priest could go. The ark of the covenant was kept in the Holy of Holies.

Stonemasons shaped blocks of limestone before using them in the building of the temple.

A plumb line (a line with a lead weight) was hung to make sure that the bronze pillars stood straight.

Workmen probably used cranes and scaffolding in the construction of the temple.

A hone for sharpening tools

A bowdrill for making holes

Nails

# The Visit of the Queen of Sheba

Solomon dreamed that God told him to make a wish and whatever it was it would be granted. Solomon replied, "I am your servant and you have made me king in place of my father David. I am king over your chosen people, so give me the wisdom to rule your people and know the difference between right and wrong." God was pleased with Solomon and replied, "Because you have asked for this, and nothing for yourself, I will make you wise and also give you wealth and a long life."

One day two women came to Solomon to settle their argument. One of the women explained the problem: "This woman and I live in the same house. I had a baby boy, then three days later she had a baby boy. During the night this woman's son died

because she lay on him. So she got up in the middle of the night and took my son while I was asleep. She put him in bed with her and put her dead baby in my bed. The next morning I found my son was dead! Then when I looked more closely I realized he was not my son at all."

At this point the second woman said, "No! The living one is my son. Yours is dead." Solomon turned away and asked for a sword. He then said, "Cut the living child in two and give one half to this woman and the other half to that woman." The first woman, who was the real mother of the boy, was filled with horror and cried, "Please give her the child. Don't kill him!"

*Solomon imported purple-dyed cloth from Phoenicia. The Phoenicians lived along the coast and obtained the purple dye from a special sea-snail, called a murex.*

*A murex shell*

*Egyptian jewelry, such as this necklace (left), and Phoenician glass vessels (right) were prized objects. They are the sort of goods that Solomon would have bought.*

*Solomon's merchant ships traded with countries in Asia and Africa. The king had a special interest in exotic animals and plants from faraway countries. From Asia he brought peacocks, apes, and baboons. He also collected many different plants to use as spices and perfumes.*

*A patas monkey*

*A peacock*

*Spikenard, a spice used to perfume oils*

But the other woman said, "Neither I nor you shall have him. Cut him in two." Then Solomon said: "Give the living baby to the first woman. Do not kill him. She is his mother."

News of Solomon's wisdom soon spread far and wide. People came from all over the world to listen to him.

A very powerful queen from the country of Sheba in the south of Arabia heard of Solomon's fame. She decided to travel to Jerusalem. She arrived with hundreds of camels carrying spices, gold, and precious stones. She talked with Solomon and he was able to answer all the questions she asked him. She had never seen such wealth nor spoken with someone so wise before, though she was known for her riches and wisdom.

Solomon had never met anyone as beautiful as the Queen of Sheba before. They spent some time together, and then she returned to her country.

*Solomon's empire (bordered by the red line) stretched from the Euphrates River in the north to the Red Sea. The empire later split into two kingdoms which were called Israel and Judah.*

*A camel caravan*

TIGRIS RIVER

EUPHRATES RIVER

MEDITERRANEAN SEA

ISRAEL

Jerusalem

JUDAH

EGYPT

RED SEA

Nile River

ARABIA

Route of the Queen of Sheba

SHEBA

# THE TIME OF THE PROPHETS

*Ivory comb*

*Ivory bedhead*

***Stories foreshadowing a
nation's fall***

## Jezebel and the Palace of Ivory

The death of King Solomon weakened the empire of the Israelites. Solomon and David had both come from the kingdom of Judah in the south. The people there expected that their future king would also come from Judah. But the people of Israel, the northern kingdom which included the ten northern tribes, wanted their own king.

Israel rebelled and set up a capital at Samaria to rival Jerusalem in Judah.

Samaria grew to be a prosperous city. One king of Israel, Ahab, was married to Jezebel, a Phoenician princess. The Phoenicians were a seafaring people, known for their skill at ivory carving. Ahab built a spectacular palace decorated with ivory for his wife. Ivory was an expensive luxury, and the people of Israel suffered the

*An ivory plaque of a sphinx carved by Phoenician craftsmen. A sphinx was a mythical creature with the head of a man, the body of a lion, and hawk's wings.*

*Asherah*

*Astarte*

*Rashef*

A bronze statue of Baal, the chief of the Canaanite gods. He was also worshiped by the Phoenicians. People believed that Baal could command the thunder and lightning.

El

These figures (called idols) represent gods of other religions practiced at this time. The Israelites copied many of the customs of their neighbors and some followed their religions, too.

hardships of high taxes in order to pay for Jezebel's palace. The Phoenician craftsmen who built the palace grew rich while the people of Israel became poorer. The prophets (who interpreted the word of God) saw the ivory palace as an example of the selfish and extravagant behavior of Ahab and Jezebel.

Jezebel was a powerful and ruthless queen. When she married Ahab, she continued to worship the Phoenician gods, whose chief was called Baal. She built altars to these gods, where many people of Israel soon came to worship.

The priests of Judah became worried that the people of Israel, this powerful kingdom, were no longer worshiping the real God who had led them out of Egypt and given them their laws. They knew that only disaster could come of this. So Elijah, the most forceful and fiery of the prophets, issued a challenge.

Two wooden altars were set up, one for Baal, and one for God. The followers of Baal prayed to their god to set fire to his altar—but nothing happened. Elijah was so confident in his faith that when his turn came, he poured water over the altar three times so that it would be difficult to light. He then prayed to God, and the altar instantly burst into flames.

This ivory carving comes from Nimrud in Assyria. It shows a woman at a window wearing an Egyptian wig. Fragments of ivory with this same design were found at Jezebel's palace.

# Jonah and the Great Fish

A powerful new kingdom, Assyria, arose in the east. The Assyrians depicted their battle victories in wall carvings in their palaces. Visitors to their cities, including the capital at Nineveh, saw these carved pictures of prisoners hanging from poles or impaled on stakes. When they returned home they spread fear with their tales of the ferocious and cruel Assyrians.

The stories of the Assyrians reached Israel and the prophet Jonah. God told him, "Go at once to the great city of Nineveh and speak out against it. I have heard of its wickedness." Jonah was terrified by God's command and fled to the port of Joppa on the Mediterranean coast, where he boarded a ship, hoping to escape from God.

Soon after the boat set sail, a storm blew up and threatened to wreck it. In a panic, the crew threw the cargo overboard to lighten the ship, but it was no use. They prayed to their own gods for help, but the storm still raged on. They decided to draw lots to find out whose wicked deed was responsible for the gods' anger and this storm. The lot fell on Jonah. He told them that he was an Israelite running away from God and the storm was his fault. "Throw me overboard and the sea will become calm," Jonah told the ship's crew.

The men felt sorry for Jonah and tried to row back to land, but the sea grew

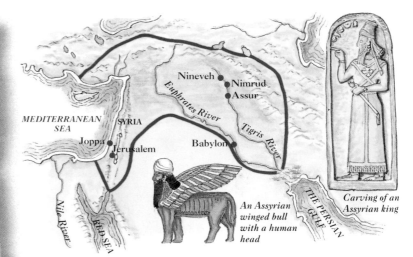

*An Assyrian winged bull with a human head*

*Carving of an Assyrian king*

*A map of the Assyrian Empire (bordered by the red line). The empire dominated the Near East from about 900 to 600 B.C.E.*

*The inside of an Assyrian palace at Nimrud on the Tigris River. The walls were decorated with pictures of foreign kings and nobles paying taxes to the Assyrians. Huge statues of winged lions with human heads stood proudly in the hall of the palace.*

This Assyrian wall carving shows prisoners being led away, possibly to be tortured. Assyrian kings had conquered peoples transported to different parts of their empire to work as slaves.

through all this, when nothing will be done to these people? Jonah thought to himself. He sat down outside the city to see what would happen.

God made a vine grow over his head for shade, which pleased Jonah. But the next day a worm chewed the vine and it withered. Jonah complained to God, and God replied, "You are concerned about this vine, yet you did not tend it or make it grow. It sprang up overnight and died overnight. But Nineveh has more than a hundred and twenty thousand people who cannot tell the difference between right and wrong. Should I not be concerned about them?" And so God showed his mercy to the people of Nineveh because they had repented.

wilder. In the end they threw Jonah overboard, and the wind and rain died down instantly. As Jonah sank into the depths of the sea, he was swallowed by a great fish. He stayed in its stomach for three days and nights, praying to God for forgiveness the whole time. At the end of the three days the fish vomited Jonah onto dry land, where he lay exhausted and fell asleep.

God's message came to Jonah again: "Go to the wicked city of Nineveh." Jonah awoke and was happy now to obey God. He walked the streets of Nineveh, shouting, "Forty more days and Nineveh will be destroyed." To his surprise, the Assyrians believed him. The king took off his robes and covered himself with sackcloth. He knelt down in the dust and prayed to God for forgiveness. All the people of the city fasted for forty days and prayed with their king.

Even though the people had repented, Jonah was angry when God did not destroy Nineveh. Why was I put

A reconstruction of the Assyrians capturing the city of Lachish near Jerusalem. The powerful Assyrian army included archers and men with slings and spears. Battering rams were used to try to knock down the city walls.

# The Fall of Israel

When Assyrian rulers conquered other countries they stole their treasures and forced the people to pay taxes. In the middle of the ninth century B.C.E., twelve kings of conquered countries, including Ahab of Israel, united to fight against the powerful Assyrian Empire. But they were defeated and had to pay taxes to the emperor. Still, most of these small countries were left alone by the Assyrians and allowed to keep their lands.

However, in 745 B.C.E. the Assyrian emperor Tiglath-pileser (known as Pul in the Bible) wanted more. When Tiglath-pileser conquered Syria he took complete control of its lands. Neighboring rulers panicked. King Menahem of Israel tried to pay off Tiglath-pileser with a thousand talents (weights) of silver and was allowed to keep his lands for a while. But soon Israel lost the lands of Galilee and Gilead in the north to Assyria. When

Shalmaneser came to the Assyrian throne, the new Israelite king, Hoshea, tried to persuade the Egyptians to join him in a rebellion against Assyria.

The Pharaoh of Egypt was not interested, nor were any of Israel's old allies. Israel was alone in the rebellion. Hoshea was

**MAKING A WOOLEN GARMENT**
*The shearer cut the wool from the coats of his sheep. The wool was then washed and dyed.*

*Shearing scissors*

*The wool was straightened with a metal comb.*

*HOUSEHOLD ITEMS*

*An oil lamp*

*A stone flour mill*

captured, and Israel surrendered its lands until only the capital, Samaria, remained. Samaria held out for nearly two years before it, too, was forced to surrender to the Assyrians.

Shalmaneser died at about this time, and the new emperor, Sargon, took 27,290 Israelites as prisoners. This was the end of the northern kingdom of Israel. The Assyrians made Samaria part of their empire and people from Syria, Babylon, and Arabia went to live there. The Israelites who went into Assyria disappeared from history, and became known as the ten lost tribes of Israel.

*A reconstruction of an Israelite home from the northern kingdom of Israel just before the Assyrian invasion. The walls were made of stone and covered with mud-plaster. The entrance led to a courtyard, which was used as an open-air kitchen. Living rooms and rooms for cattle opened off the courtyard. At the back of the house was another large living room with a ladder leading up to sleeping quarters. A second ladder led to the roof, where grain and oil could be stored in large jars.*

*Threads of wool were fed onto a spindle and spun into balls of yarn.*

*Most houses would have had a loom like this one to weave the yarn into rugs or clothing.*

*A bread oven*

*A strainer*

*A bronze whisk*

# Hezekiah's Troubles

A simple sundial made by placing a stick in the ground

An Egyptian sundial

*When Hezekiah became very ill he prayed to God. The shadow on the palace sundial moved backward as a sign from God that he would live for another fifteen years. Sundials use the shadow cast by the sun to tell the time.*

Isaiah was a priest in the Temple of Jerusalem and one of the greatest prophets who ever lived. He was married to a prophetess and had two sons. Because of his special relationship with God, he could see into the future and he advised the kings of Judah what they should to do.

Isaiah warned King Ahaz of Judah that what had just happened to Israel could also happen to Judah. He said that although Ahaz paid taxes to the Assyrians, the mighty empire of Assyria could cut down Judah as easily as a razor cuts through a beard. But Ahaz wouldn't listen, nor would he stop worshiping and promoting pagan gods.

When Ahaz's son Hezekiah came to the throne of Judah, at the age of twenty-five, Isaiah told him to follow the true religion of his kingdom. Hezekiah obeyed him, destroying the pagan temples in Judah and inviting the citizens of Judah and conquered Israel to come to Jerusalem to celebrate the Passover feast. He did this in the belief that God would save the kingdom of Judah from the Assyrians.

But it was too late. King Sennacherib of Assyria and his army began to move quickly from the north, conquering one city after another. They

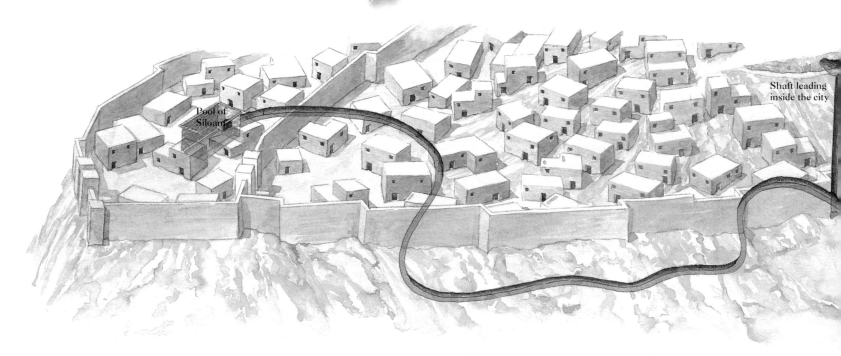

Pool of Siloam

Shaft leading inside the city

captured the city of Lachish, only thirty miles from Jerusalem.

King Hezekiah was so worried about Sennacherib's invasion that he developed a terrible boil. Isaiah ordered hot figs on a cloth to be laid on the boil. This was done and Hezekiah instantly recovered. Various other remedies were used for different illnesses in the ancient world, including oils, lotions, and balms. Still, Isaiah's treatment was unusual because most disease or illness was thought to be brought on by a sin. People believed that the only cure for illness was to stop sinning.

Hezekiah began to panic at the advance of the Assyrians. Against Isaiah's advice he asked the Egyptians for help. But the Egyptians did not come to his aid.

Remembering how the people of Samaria had died of hunger and thirst,

*An Assyrian king on a hunting expedition. The king is about to throw his spear, while a charioteer controls the horses and a servant stands by with more weapons. Lion hunting was a favorite sport of Assyrian kings.*

Spring of Gihon

*Hezekiah's tunnel diverted fresh water for a third of a mile underneath the city. Two sets of diggers tunneled toward each other from the opposite ends of the tunnel. The men called out to each other as they dug to make sure that their two short tunnels would meet to form one long tunnel.*

Hezekiah decided to build an underground tunnel to give the people of Jerusalem a water supply within the city walls. The tunnel would carry water from the Spring of Gihon outside the gates of Jerusalem to the Pool of Siloam inside the walls. The tunnel diggers managed to carve 1,748 feet through the earth with very simple tools, an amazing feat of engineering.

Meanwhile, the Assyrians threatened to destroy Jerusalem if Hezekiah did not surrender. Isaiah assured him that God would not let Jerusalem fall to the Assyrians. Then, strangely, overnight, a hundred and eighty-five thousand of the Assyrian soldiers who were camped nearby suddenly died. No one knows what happened to the soldiers; it was a complete mystery.

Though Hezekiah was forced to continue paying taxes to the Assyrians, the city of Jerusalem was saved as Isaiah had foretold.

# The Burning of Jerusalem

Over a hundred years after the Assyrians destroyed Samaria, a new empire called Babylon arose east of the Euphrates River. With Babylon to the east and Egypt to the west, the small kingdom of Judah had to form an alliance with one of these empires to gain protection.

Judah first allied itself to Babylon. But after it was invaded by Pharaoh Neco of Egypt, Judah had to switch its allegiance to Egypt. This enraged Nebuchadnezzar, the king of Babylon, and he ordered an invasion of Judah. When the king of Judah surrendered, Nebuchadnezzar made Zedekiah Judah's new king.

The prophet Jeremiah warned Zedekiah not to rebel against Babylon, for he could not expect help from Egypt. The king's only hope was to trust in God. But Zedekiah wouldn't listen and planned to overthrow the Babylonians. When Nebuchadnezzar heard this, he ordered his entire army to attack the city of Jerusalem. The people of Jerusalem believed that God lived in the Temple and that he would protect his city. But Jeremiah again predicted disaster, saying the Israelites were no longer deserving of God's protection.

Jeremiah was thrown in prison and the people of Jerusalem prepared for

*WEAPONS OF SIEGE WARFARE*
*A siege engine with battering ram*

*The battering ram was a long iron or wooden pole suspended from a rope. It was swung into the city's walls by soldiers who were inside the siege engine.*

*A pointed ram for pushing into cracks in the wall*

*A blunt ram for breaking sections of the wall*

*BABYLONIAN WEAPONS*

*A bronze ax head*

*A bow and quiver*

the siege. After a year and a half the food ran out. Zedekiah tried to escape, but he was captured and taken to Babylon. The Babylonians burned Jerusalem to the ground, and nearly all the people of Judah were taken to Babylon.

*An attacking army would surround the city and try to cut off the water and food supply in order to starve the people into surrender. Then they would try to get through the city walls either by tunneling under them or, if they were made of wood, by setting them alight. They would also set light to the wooden city gates. Ramps of stones, logs, and trodden-down earth would be made to get over the walls. The tops of the walls were usually weaker, and easier to break.*

*Defenders threw flaming torches from the top of the walls to try and set the wooden battering rams alight.*

*Some attackers had long arching shields to protect their heads from arrows. Others would put ladders up against the walls and try to climb over them.*

*A mace, a heavy club*

*A shield*

67

# THE EXILE

*Plants from the gardens of Babylon*

*Stories of the exile to foreign lands and the rebirth of a nation*

## Life in Babylon

Some people, including Jeremiah, fled from Judah and eventually found haven in Egypt, but about twenty thousand men, women, and children were taken captive. King Nebuchadnezzar forced his prisoners to walk over eight hundred miles to Babylon on the Euphrates River.

Babylon was well known as one of the most beautiful cities in the ancient world. The first thing the tired and hungry people of Judah saw when they arrived was a huge, magnificent blue gateway decorated with bulls and dragons. Inside the gates were "hanging gardens" of exotic trees, and splendid palaces. Although Babylonian kings and soldiers had a reputation for being cruel, the ordinary inhabitants of Babylon welcomed the people of Jerusalem and treated them well. They settled in an area south of the main city, called Nippur, and here they followed the advice Jeremiah had sent to captives in Babylon before the time of Jerusalem's destruction: "Build houses and live in them, plant gardens and eat their fruit, marry and have sons and daughters."

Most of them took up the work they had done in Judah, such as farming and carpentry. Others became shopkeepers for the first time, buying and selling goods. Babylon was a busy city, ten times the size of Jerusalem. On the streets and squares, between massive temples to strange gods, life was noisy and colorful. Camel caravans, donkeys pulling carts, priests, pilgrims, and traders flooded down the main highways. The temple authorities in Babylon ran their own stores and warehouses. Banks and chambers of commerce fixed the prices of goods sold along the Euphrates River.

Although an ancient city, Babylon gave the modern world a model for an "exchange"—a business center in which prices and markets are controlled.

*A broad, paved road led up to the main entrance of Babylon, the Ishtar gate. Bulls and dragons made of bricks decorated the high walls on either side. During festivals, great processions of people passed through the gateway, carrying statues of their gods.*

*The Hanging Gardens of Babylon were one of the seven wonders of the ancient world. Nebuchadnezzar planted terraces of trees in the high courtyards of his palaces. One story says that he created the gardens for a foreign princess, to remind her of her homeland.*

69

# Psalms and Music

For hundreds of years, from before the time of King David until after the Exile, the Hebrew people wrote and sang poems to tell of great disasters and to celebrate times of joy. These musical poems are called psalms and were sung at festivals and on special occasions to glorify God and to remind the Israelites of their history. Now that the people of Judah (or Jews, as they became known) no longer had a homeland, they wrote psalms about their past, looking back to the days when David ruled their nation. Much of the Jews' great poetry can be found in the psalms.

*A fragment of the Dead Sea scrolls, which were found in a cave at Qumran near the Dead Sea in 1947 by a shepherd boy. The scrolls were hidden in jars and placed inside the cave. They are the oldest surviving copy of the Hebrew Bible, including the psalms.*

*Music was arranged for the choir and orchestra of Levite priests who sang and played in the Jerusalem Temple. The instruments the priests played included cymbals, lyres, harps, and trumpets.*

*The lyre (the instrument that looks like a harp) and the shofar (the trumpet-like instrument) were played in biblical times.*

King David organized the Levite singers and orchestra and wrote seventy-three of the psalms. While there was much to celebrate in his day, many of the songs written during the captivity in Babylon had sad themes:

> By the rivers of Babylon we sat
>     and wept
>     when we remembered Zion
>     (Jerusalem).
> There on the poplar trees
>     we hung our harps,
>     for there our captors asked us
>     for songs.
> [Psalm 137]

The singing was always meant for God. People sang with joy when they wanted to thank God for helping them in times of need, and they sang with sadness when they felt alone, rejected, and unable to understand God's ways:

> We have heard with our ears,
>     O God;
>     our fathers have told us
> what you did in their days,

in days long ago.
With your hand you drove out
    the nations
    and planted our fathers...
Through you we push back our
    enemies;
    through your name we
    trample our foes...
But now you have rejected us;
    you no longer go out with
    our armies...
You gave us up to be
    devoured like sheep
    and have scattered us
    among the nations...
We are brought down to the dust;
    our bodies cling to the ground.
Awake, O God! Why do you sleep?
    Rouse yourself! Do not reject
    us for ever.
[Psalm 44]

*In Psalm 44 the Israelites lament that they are defeated. The Israelites considered bowing a form of idol worship, and so a sin, but it was a common practice for other biblical peoples. In this Egyptian relief, people bow down before an official.*

71

# Belshazzar's Feast

The empire of Babylon grew quickly under King Nebuchadnezzar. But the power became too much for him and he went mad. He became like a beast, sitting outside in the pouring rain and eating grass.

Three kings came and went in the next seven years, but none was able to rule the empire. Two powerful nations, the Medes and the Persians, threatened to attack any day. But the Babylonians continued their grand ways as if nothing were wrong.

One such Babylonian was Prince Belshazzar. At a feast he held for a thousand guests, Belshazzar was drinking wine from the gold and silver goblets that Nebuchadnezzar had taken from the Temple at Jerusalem. Suddenly he looked at one wall of his banqueting room in disbelief. A hand without a body was writing a message on the wall: "Mene, mene, tekel, u'pharsin."

Belshazzar's legs gave way and he fell to the floor with fear. None of his wise men could understand the writing. The queen told him that a Jew named Daniel was at court and would be able to help. Daniel was summoned to reveal the meaning of the words: Mene (measure): "The days of your reign are numbered;

## WEIGHTS AND MEASURES

*Scales balanced precious stones against stones of a known weight.*

Bronze lion-weights like these from Assyria were used to value different amounts of goods. Weights came in the form of many living creatures including lions, ducks, frogs, and insects.

## PRECIOUS STONES AND METALS

*Diamond*

*Turquoise*

*Lapis lazuli*

God will bring your kingdom to an end."

Tekel (weight): "You have been weighed on the scales and are found wanting."

U'pharsin (divide): "Your kingdom will be divided and given to the Medes and the Persians."

As a reward, Belshazzar made Daniel the third-highest official in the land. But that night, the Medes invaded and Belshazzar was killed.

*The quay alongside the Euphrates River was outside the walls of Babylon. Ships loaded with gold, silver, spices, and other precious goods arrived every day. Coins were not used to trade between different nations, so prices had to be agreed on in terms of a weight of gold or silver. The words on the wall at Belshazzar's feast were three weights: mene (mina), tekel (shekel), and u'pharsin (fraction). A mina was equal to sixty shekels. A fraction was a division of a weight.*

*Bath measures were used for measuring liquid goods such as wine and oil. There were different sizes for different amounts of liquid. The largest was the donkey-load, or kor.*

*Solid goods such as cereals were measured in large containers. An ephah was large enough to hold a woman. An omer was a tenth of an ephah.*

*An ephah*

*An omer*

*Mother-of-pearl*

*Gold*

*Ruby*

*Silver*

# Queen Esther

It was soon the turn of the Persians to attack Babylon. They cleverly diverted the Euphrates River and marched into the city along its now dry river bed. After Babylon was defeated, many Jews went to live in Susa, the capital of the Persian Empire, where they soon rose to high positions in the government and the army. It was a quiet time when Jews and other foreigners were free to live as they pleased. Greek doctors, Babylonian astronomers, and Phoenician explorers all lived and worked together peacefully.

When Xerxes (called Ahasuerus in the Bible) was emperor of Persia, a beauty contest was held to find him a new queen. He chose Esther, an orphan who

*This is a gold bracelet belonging to a Persian queen. Gold captured from the enemies of the Persians was melted down and made into new jewelry by Persian craftsmen.*

*A Persian guard. The Persian king had a royal bodyguard of a thousand men. These men were called "the Immortals" (people who never die) because whenever one of them fell in battle there was always another one to replace him. This guard is wearing a rope headband, leather boots, and fine clothes. His long spear is tipped with silver.*

had been raised by her cousin Mordecai. An official named Haman hated the Jews and Mordecai and plotted to kill them. He persuaded Xerxes, who did not know that Esther was a Jew, that the Jews were dangerous and should all be destroyed. By drawing lots he decided that the thirteenth day of that month was the day all Jews would be killed.

Mordecai asked Esther to try to persuade the king not to allow this terrible thing. But Esther was scared, for she knew that by law anyone who approached the king unsummoned would be killed. Despite her fear, Esther approached Xerxes, but only to ask him and Haman to dinner.

At this dinner, she asked them to come again the next day. That night Xerxes decided to honor a man who had once saved his life. He meant to honor Mordecai, but Haman, who had started

74

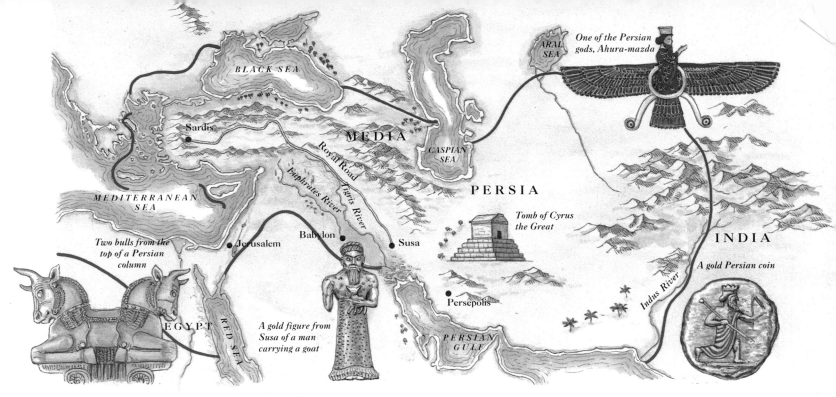

*The Persian Empire (bordered by the red line) was larger than the Assyrian and Babylonian empires. It stretched from India to Egypt. The Persian king appointed governors to control each province (area) in his empire.*

building the gallows on which to hang Mordecai, thought Xerxes was going to honor him. When Xerxes asked Haman to dress Mordecai in fine robes and escort him on horseback through the city, Haman was disgraced.

At Esther's second dinner, she told Xerxes of Haman's plot to kill the Jews—and that

*A statue of the Persian king Darius I, father of Xerxes. Darius was an excellent general who built roads, such as the Royal Road, all over his empire to ensure fast communication between himself and his subjects.*

the Jews were her people. Xerxes stormed out in a rage. Terrified, Haman threw himself at Esther and begged for mercy. When Xerxes returned to see Haman sprawled over his queen, he could not control his anger. He ordered Haman to be hanged on the very gallows that had been built for Mordecai.

By law, Xerxes could not withdraw his order to kill the Jews. But at Esther's request he made a law allowing Jews to protect themselves and their property on that day. To celebrate the law, the Jews held a feast called Purim, named after "Pur," the Hebrew word for "lot," in memory of the lot drawn to decide the date for the execution of the Jews. Purim, the Jews' most joyous holiday, is still celebrated today.

*Silver and gold coins depicting kings of Persia.*

# The Return to Jerusalem

This clay barrel records some of the things Cyrus the Great did when he became king. It describes how he allowed Jewish temples to be rebuilt.

I n the first year of Persian rule over Babylon, Cyrus the Great allowed the exiled Jews to return home. Over forty-two thousand people set off on the long journey back to Jerusalem. Priests led the long caravan, while two hundred singers kept up the spirits of the men, women, and children who followed slowly behind. After arriving in Haran, they took the same route Abraham had walked one thousand four hundred years before. Eventually the long-awaited day arrived. Amid the brown hills of Judah they saw the ruins of Jerusalem.

The new arrivals started to rebuild the city and the Temple. But with no homes and little to eat, people soon became more concerned with their own needs. They also had to face attacks from their northern neighbors, the Samaritans. These people were Jews who had not been taken into captivity when the Assyrians conquered Israel. They too felt the land belonged to them.

News of these troubles reached Nehemiah, who was the cupbearer to the Persian king. He was an important official, and he persuaded the king to make him governor of Judah so that he could help to

An aerial view of the city of Jerusalem showing the walls which Nehemiah built to keep the city's inhabitants safe from attack. The walls enclosed the old site of Solomon's Temple and David's city. Solomon's Temple was also rebuilt by Nehemiah and the returning exiles.

sort out their problems. He set off from Babylon with a team of builders and rebuilt the city walls.

But defense of the city was not the only problem. The people of Jerusalem were not following the laws God had given Moses. Many had forgotten their history and did not even know the laws. Others were marrying foreign wives and did not speak Hebrew, which was the language of Moses' law. They needed a leader like Moses to show them once again how to live as God wanted.

The man who did this was Ezra, a priest living in Persia. When he came to Jerusalem, all the city assembled in the Temple court. From dawn till noon Ezra

*After the time of Ezra scribes became important teachers of the law of Moses. Scribes also performed social functions such as recording business transactions and writing letters for people.*

read out the law from his scroll. As he read, his scribes (priests who interpret the laws) translated the scripture into Aramaic so the people could understand, and explained the law. The people listened carefully, and gradually they realized how wrongly they were living. They felt ashamed and asked for forgiveness. But at the same time they were glad that they had found the way to follow God.

All Jews in every part of the ancient Near East could now believe they were again one people. They might live in different countries, but they all shared the law of Moses.

*This is how a Jewish synagogue in Persia at about this time may have looked. Synagogues were places of worship. They were built by Jews who lived in foreign countries where there was no Temple of Jerusalem.*

# Index

Page numbers in *italics* refer to illustrations and maps.